WRITERS AND CRITICS

Chief Editor

A. NORMAN JEFFARES

Advisory Editors

DAVID DAICHES   C. P. SNOW

HENRY JAMES's position among the novelists of the world is now higher than it has ever been, but not enough people realise how much pleasure his work can give them. In abstract discussions of his techniques and themes the sheer wit and eloquence of his writing can easily be missed. In this study Douglas Jefferson aims at providing a sympathetic introduction to his work as a whole, with some account of the viewpoints of his more important critics. The "Americanism" of James, especially in his approach to Europe, is stressed as a major source of interest. Douglas Jefferson, a Senior Lecturer at the University of Leeds, has edited the *Pelican Book of Eighteenth Century Prose* and written on Sterne and Goldsmith, and other novelists. He is deeply interested in the nineteenth-century American novel and is at present writing a study of Henry James's idea of place.

HENRY JAMES

D. W. JEFFERSON

OLIVER AND BOYD
EDINBURGH AND LONDON

OLIVER AND BOYD LTD
Tweeddale Court
Edinburgh 1

39A Welbeck Street
London W. 1

First published 1960

Printed in Great Britain for Oliver and Boyd Ltd
by Robert MacLehose and Co. Ltd, Glasgow.

CONTENTS

DEDICATION

For

My Father and Mother

ACKNOWLEDGMENTS

Acknowledgments are due to the Trustees of Henry James's Estate and to John Farquharson Ltd for permission to reproduce all matter quoted from Henry James's works.

Acknowledgments are also due to the following for permission to make quotations from the works mentioned: Jonathan Cape Ltd (Percy Lubbock, *The Craft of Fiction*; Elizabeth Robins, *Theatre and Friendship*); Chatto and Windus Ltd (M. Bewley, *The Complex Fate*; F. R. Leavis, *The Great Tradition*); Rupert Hart-Davis Ltd (L. Edel, *The Untried Years*); The Oxford University Press (F. O. Matthiessen, *Henry James: The Major Phase*); and Mr Edmund Wilson (*The Triple Thinkers*).

The photograph on the front cover is reproduced by permission of E. O. Hoppé

ABBREVIATED TITLES
BY WHICH HENRY JAMES'S WORKS
ARE CITED IN THE TEXT

Am.	=	*The American.*
Amb.	=	*The Ambassadors.*
B.	=	*The Bostonians.*
D.M.	=	*Daisy Miller* etc. (St. edn.).
E.H.	=	*English Hours.*
G.B.	=	*The Golden Bowl.*
H.J.A.	=	*Henry James: Autobiography*, ed. F. W. Dupee, 1956, containing *A Small Boy and Others*, *Notes of a Son and a Brother*, *The Middle Years*.
L.	=	*The Letters of Henry James*, ed. Percy Lubbock, 2 vols. 1920.
L.B.	=	*Lady Barbarina* etc. (St. edn.)
L.M.	=	*The Lesson of the Master* etc. ("Chiltern Library," John Lehmann), containing also "The Death of the Lion" and "The Coxon Fund".
P.C.	=	*The Princess Casamassima.*
P.L.	=	*The Portrait of a Lady.*
R.	=	*The Reverberator*, etc. (St. edn.), containing also "A Passionate Pilgrim," "The Madonna of the Future," and "Madame de Mauves."
R.H.	=	*Roderick Hudson.*
S.P.	=	*The Spoils of Poynton.*
S.S.	=	*Selected Stories of Henry James*, selected by G. Hopkins, Worlds Classics, O.U.P. 1957, containing "The Real Thing," "The Private Life," "Broken Wings," and "The Two Faces."
T.M.	=	*The Tragic Muse.*
W.D.	=	*The Wings of the Dove.*
W.M.K.	=	*What Maisie Knew.*
W.W.S.	=	*William Wetmore Story and his Friends.*

OTHER ABBREVIATED TITLES

G.T.	=	F. R. Leavis, *The Great Tradition.*
Q.H.J.	=	*The Question of Henry James*, ed. F. W. Dupee.

CHAPTER I

EARLY YEARS:
JAMES'S BACKWARD GLANCE

We are indeed fortunate in having James's imaginative reconstruction of the first thirty years or so of his life in *A Small Boy and Others* (1913), *Notes of a Son and a Brother* (1914) and the fragment published posthumously as *The Middle Years* (1917). In spite of much ill-health during the time of their composition, these books are among his best works. All writers on his early period are obliged to draw heavily upon them, with the sober realisation that their many fine passages will be somewhat less effective in quotation than in the full amplitude of their context. Perhaps the most useful way to begin this brief sketch of his career is with a passage long enough to give a sustained impression of the quality of these childhood memories. Passing over for the moment those facts about his family and background which James himself reserves for more effective use at a later stage in his narrative, we start with the "small boy" himself in the New York where he was born in 1843. It is characteristic of these writings that they should be richly evocative of the places in which his impressionable years were spent. In one of the more piquant of the early descriptions he recalls "the rank and rubbishy waterside quarters" with which, as a "safely-prowling infant," he was familiar, "where groceries . . . largely of the 'green' order, so far as greenness could persist in the torrid air," together with "carts and barrows and boxes and baskets," lay scattered about in splendid disorder:

Why the throb of romance should have beat time for me to such visions I can scarce explain, or can explain only by the fact that the squalor was a squalor wonderfully mixed and seasoned, and that I should wrong the whole impression if I didn't figure it first and foremost as that of some vast succulent cornucopia. What did the stacked boxes and baskets of our youth represent but the boundless fruitage of that more bucolic age of the American world, and what was after all of so strong an assault as the rankness of such a harvest?[1]

One is reminded of the great mountains of vegetables in Zola's novel about the Parisian markets, *Le Ventre de Paris*. James's imagination was much finer and more genial than Zola's, but both writers had a taste for the prodigious. The passage continues with rich memories of the fruit-eating of his early years:

Where is that fruitage now, where in particular are the peaches *d'antan*? where the mounds of Isabella grapes and Seckel pears in the sticky sweetness of which our childhood seems to have been steeped?... Above all the public heaps of them, the high-piled receptacles at every turn, touched the street as with a sort of southern plenty; the note of the rejected and scattered fragments, the memory of the slippery skins and rinds and kernels with which the old dislocated flags were bestrown, is itself endeared to me and contributes a further pictorial grace. We ate everything in those days by the bushel and the barrel, as from stores that were infinite; we handled water-melons as freely as cocoanuts, and the amount of stomach-ache involved was negligible in the general Eden-like consciousness.

Passages like this are our best introduction to James. No writer has ever been better equipped to convey the note of enjoyment and well-being. Whether he is remembering the "bedizened saucers [of ice-cream] heaped up for our fond consumption,"[2] after visits to the dentist, or the "finer vibrations" experienced when he "stood long and drank deep at those founts of romance that gushed from the huge placards of the theatre,"[3] these autobiographical pages testify lavishly to the joys of childhood. James's capacity for enjoyment, at many levels including the most elementary, and his delight in expressing it are perhaps the first things about him that are worth knowing.

One of the purposes of the autobiographies was to recapture the experiences which illustrate the emergence of his powers of perception. In his references to himself as a "mere mite of observation," or to the "small straining vision" exercised in his earliest discriminations, he achieves a tone of humorous tenderness which preserves these books from the taint of the egotistical. They are so written that we never lose awareness of the processes of memory and reflexion by which they are sustained. Some things are more clearly remembered than others. In passages describing the theatrical entertainments of his boyhood, he draws upon a remarkable wealth of treasured detail. The very immaturity of the small boy caused many of his perceptions to be incomplete and uncertain, and where the materials of memory become faint or baffling, the speculative mind of the writer supplies its own order, sometimes with difficulty for him and for us.

His extraordinary father, the philosopher and associate of Emerson and other writers of that generation, is not described until we reach *Notes of a Son and a Brother*, but something of his outlook and personality is reflected in the earlier reminiscences, notably in the general freedom from constraint that strikes one from the outset as characteristic of James's home life. Henry James senior had liberated himself from the strict Calvinism of his formidable father, an immigrant from Ireland whose energies in business built up the fortune on which the material well-being of the family was to rest. His freedom was not achieved without cost: there were years of uncertainty and anxiety, culminating in the horrific psychological experience which he came to refer to, in Swedenborgian terms, as the "vastation." The teachings of Swedenborg played their part in restoring him to spiritual health, and eventually he developed a very personal philosophy, the most relevant features of which were an exceedingly generous view of man's natural powers and faculties in relation to the Divine scheme. In his admirable description of his father—it is one of the greatest of filial tributes—Henry James junior does not claim to have understood this philosophy; but he may be said to have *felt* it—that is, as it manifested itself in his generous and sympathetic personality: "I only thought of it as something very good and fine founded on those forces in him that came home to us and that touched us all the while."[4] If he did not digest the intellectual content of his father's ideas, he responded to his "tone": ". . . one may fairly say his philosophy *was* his tone." A horror of priggishness and pedantic moralising was one of his father's marked characteristics. The James family were brought up without experience of conventional religion, and Henry James confesses that for him clergymen were "creatures of pure hearsay" until he began to discover this romantic species in the novels of George Eliot and Trollope.[5]

James's mother, an ex-Calvinist converted to her husband's unorthodox outlook, is the subject of a splendid passage:

> To have attempted any projection of our father's aspect without an immediate reference to her sovereign care for him and for all of us as the so widely open, yet so softly enclosing, lap of all his liberties and all our securities, all our variety and withal our harmony, the harmony that was for nine-tenths of it our sense of her gathered life in us, and of her having no other—to have so proceeded has been but to defer by instinct and by

scruple to the kind of truth and of beauty before which the direct report breaks down.[6]

There were five children, of whom William was the eldest, Henry being sixteen months younger. The others were named Garth Wilkinson, Robertson, and Alice. One of their father's idiosyncrasies was an inability to decide whether to have his children educated in America or in Europe. He expressed the opinion in a letter to Emerson that in Europe they might get a better "sensuous education" than at home, but the move was delayed. "Europe," of course, was a magic word. James records his first awareness of its associations in a charming passage about an early school friend in New York who, with his French accent and ways, gave

... the earliest, or at least the most personal, tap to that pointed prefigurement of the manners of 'Europe', which, inserted wedge-like, if not to say peg-like, into my young allegiance, was to split the tender organ into such unequal halves. His the toy hammer that drove in the very point of the golden nail.[7]

In 1855 the move was finally made, and Europe became an actuality. Nothing in the autobiographies is more delightful than the memory of one episode of the journey: the arrival in a French village, with a village street unlike anything he had seen before, a castle, and finally a peasant woman with a red petticoat and sabots.[8] This was a crucial moment. "It made a bridge over to more things than I then knew."

James was now to experience schools in Geneva, Paris, and Boulogne, to say nothing of tutors of different nationalities. In 1858 his father, disillusioned by European education, took them back to the United States, but after a short stay at Newport they returned, and again James went to school in Geneva. In 1860, when he was seventeen, they finally came home, settling for a short time in Newport and then in Boston. In *A Small Boy and Others* James suppressed the 1858–59 phase. As he admitted to his nephew, he was a little disturbed at the "impression of aimless vacillation" on the part of his father which the complete record might give. This irregular and much-interrupted education probably did him more good than harm. School subjects were not his strong point: he "couldn't tackle the smallest problem in mechanics or face without dismay at the blackboard the simplest geometric challenge"[9]—but he read enormously and he saw life.

Another of his father's idiosyncrasies was the wish that William and he should not narrow themselves to the extent of espousing a profession: "What we were to do instead was just to *be* something, something unconnected with specific doing, something free and uncommitted . . ."[10] It amused James that this reason should have been urged in response to William's early wish to become an artist, an ambition habitually condemned by fathers for such different reasons: that is, "as a departure from the career of business, of industry and respectability, the so-called regular life." When Henry began to write it was put to him, "with the finest bewildering eloquence . . . that this too was narrowing." Perhaps the parental preference for vagueness, though expressed with all the benignity in the world, helps to explain the purposive, professional spirit in which James applied himself to his chosen calling from the age of twenty-one.

The years before the opening of his literary career were the beginning of a period of trouble concerning which our knowledge remains very incomplete. The Civil War broke out in the spring of 1861, and later in the same year James sustained an injury as a result of being "jammed into an acute angle between two high fences,"[11] while he was lending a hand with some primitive fire-fighting apparatus. Neither he nor William, in the early months of the war, had made any move to volunteer for service,

but now Henry was physically prevented from partici-
pating. Unfortunately for his condition of mind during a
crisis so painful for the young men of his generation, the
injury could not be identified, and the surgeon whom he
consulted dismissed it as trivial. The obscurity of the case
has given rise to much conjecture, including confident
guesses relating to castration, but Leon Edel's valuable
chapter on the subject does much to clarify it.[12] His conclusion is that the evidence points to "a slipped disc, a
sacroiliac or muscular strain." For many years James
suffered from a bad back, and lamented that it had been
neglected in the early stages. What with the pain itself,
the mortification of being unable to offer an acceptable
explanation for it, and the unfortunate coincidence with
the Civil War, the years that followed were bitter for
him. It is during this phase of the story that we are obliged to recognise less happy aspects of the otherwise
splendid family to which he belonged. William also went
through a period of invalidism in his middle twenties,
when he was still unsettled in a career; their sister Alice
developed during these years the nervous symptoms from
which she was to suffer throughout her life; and the two
other brothers were also involved in ill-health. It is inevitable that biographers should inquire into the psychological aspects of these crises, but the subject is likely to
remain rather obscure. In his 1881–82 Notebook, an
autobiographical sketch, James writes feelingly of this
phase, but places the emphasis on positive things:

> It was a time of suffering so keen that that fact might
> claim to give its dark colour to the whole period; but
> this is not what I think of today . . . Ill-health, physical
> suffering, in one's younger years, is a grievous trial;
> but I am not sure that we do not bear it most easily
> then. In spite of it we feel the joy of youth . . . The
> freshness of impression and desire, the hope, the curi-
> osity, the vivacity, the sense of the richness and

mystery of the world that lies before us—there is an enchantment in all that which it takes a heavy dose of pain to quench . . .[13]

His literary career began in 1864, and by the end of 1868 he had published a dozen short stories and over fifty book reviews. He became acquainted with Lowell and Norton, and developed a close friendship with Howells, all of whom were connected with the periodicals which printed his work. What may strike the reader most about this early period is not the quality of his writing, though some pieces contain notable strokes of perception and wit, but the steady output and the evidence it gives of his determination to live by his pen. This impression may help to neutralise in some measure our feeling that he had very little to say. And too many of the stories are about defeated or perplexed young men. But with his visit to Europe in 1869, one of the important dates in his career, everything changed. It was an overwhelming and liberating experience, and from this time onwards he had a wealth of significant subject-matter.

Before we turn to this phase of his life, so rich in inspirational interest, it is valuable to bear in mind that James's friendships during the difficult Civil War years and later were such as to endear to him permanently certain American ways of living, although the specific portrayal of American manners is not carried very far in the stories of this period. In the early pages of *A Small Boy and Others* there are pleasant reminiscences of the ease and naturalness of the young people of the immediate social group in which he was brought up. "There can surely never have been anything like their good faith and, generally speaking, their sociability,"[14] he writes, and he compares them with the young people encountered later and in other places, who seemed so much "more formed and finished, more tutored and governessed, warned and armed at more points for, and no doubt often against, the social relation."[15] In a beautiful passage of *Notes of a Son and a Brother* he recalls similar qualities in the circle of friends to which he belonged in his twenties.[16] The most loved member of it was his cousin Mary (Minny) Temple, who died of tuberculosis at the age of twenty-four. James's tribute to her is a monument to qualities which, at her pitch of excellence, made her an ideal symbol of American girlhood in her time:

... 'Natural' to an effect of perfect felicity that we were never to see surpassed is what I have already praised all the Albany *cousinage* for being; but in none of the company was the note so clear as in this rarest, though at the same time symptomatically or ominously palest, flower of the stem; who was natural at more points and about more things, with a greater range of freedom and ease and reach of horizon than any of the others dreamed of.[17]

She was "the very figure and image of a felt interest in life, an interest as magnanimously far-spread, or as familiarly and exquisitely fixed, as her splendid shifting sensibility, moral, personal, nervous ... might at any moment determine." It was of the essence of her nature to become actively involved with life: "Life claimed her and used her and beset her—made her range in her groping, her naturally immature and unlighted way from beginning to end of the scale."[18] Her early death, after a courageous, agonised fight to survive, marked an epoch for Henry and William. It was "the end of their youth." It is well known that James was inspired by her memory in his portraits of two heroines, also much "beset" by life and destined for a greater range of commitment and action than Minny: Isabel Archer in *The Portrait of a Lady* and Milly Theale in *The Wings of the Dove*.

If the stories of the early period are rather limited, a letter of 1867 to his friend Thomas Sargeant Perry testifies strikingly to his sanguine hopes, not only for himself

B

but for American literature:

> ... We are Americans born—*il faut en prendre son parti.*
> I look upon it as a great blessing; and I think that to be
> an American is an excellent preparation for culture.
> We have exquisite qualities as a race, and it seems to me
> that we are ahead of the European races in the fact that
> more than either of them we can deal freely with forms
> of civilization not our own, can pick and choose and
> assimilate and in short (aesthetically etc.) claim our
> property wherever we find it ... We must of course
> have something of our own—something distinctive and
> homogeneous—and I take it that we shall find it in our
> moral consciousness, our unprecedented spiritual light-
> ness and vigour.[19]

These words may be linked with the passages about the
"circle" and Minny Temple. They may also be used as a
text for a conception of "Americanism." James was to
recognise later that the American's relationship with
Europe had many sides to it. "It's a complex fate, being
an American ...", he wrote in another letter, and his
novels and stories were to be an exploration of many different ways in which the complexity could manifest itself.

In 1869 he went to England, and then through France
and Switzerland to Italy. The much quoted letter to
William describing the "ineffable, incomparable impression of Rome," gives the full measure of his experience:

> At last—for the first time—I live! It beats everything:
> it leaves the Rome of your fancy—your education—
> nowhere ... I went reeling and moaning thro' the
> streets, in a fever of enjoyment. In the course of four or
> five hours I traversed almost the whole of Rome and
> got a glimpse of everything—the Forum, the Coliseum
> (stupendissimo!), the Pantheon, the Capitol, St.
> Peter's, the Column of Trajan, the Castle of St. Angelo
> —all the Piazzas and ruins and monuments. The effect
> is something indescribable ...[20]

There are also letters giving impressions of England and the English, and of his own compatriots abroad. James is incomparable in his genius for responding to places and to the manners of different communities. But one of his reasons for coming to Europe was ill-health, and much of his time was spent in taking treatments.

After fourteen months in Europe he spent about two years at home. Then he returned to Europe for a year and a half—his health had now improved considerably—and again he came back in 1874. In 1875 he took the decision to settle in Paris, and this gave him the opportunity to become acquainted with Parisian literary society: with Flaubert and Turgenev, in particular. He lived there until late in 1876, when he changed his mind and made his home in England.

The autobiographical record does not take us beyond the early stages of his stay in England. *The Middle Years* contains some superb impressions of the homelier aspects of English life—an eating-house, breakfast conventions, the national weather—and also of people he met, such as George Eliot and Tennyson. His encounter with the latter was an experience that demanded readjustments: the realisation that he was not Tennysonian was "like a rap on the knuckles of a sweet superstition."[21] When Tennyson read aloud his "Locksley Hall" James "heard him, in cool surprise, take even more out of his verse than he had put in."[22]

The autobiographies end at a point where James's literary life begins to be interesting to us. As we have seen, they have the great value of introducing themes which link his early life with the books he was to write: the "note of Europe"; the American girl and Minny Temple; and, of course, his own habits of perception which made the child the father of the man.

The letters of the eighteen-seventies are full of interesting reflexions on his experience of English society, into which he had been introduced in the first place through the good offices of the Nortons and others. He became a diner-out. A letter of 1877 to William describes his dining with Lord Houghton, when Gladstone, Tennyson, and Schliemann of Troy were guests. Writing to Grace Norton in 1879 he made the celebrated confession that he had dined out a hundred and seven times during the previous winter. There are descriptions of visits to Lord Rosebery's place, Mentmore, and a country house in Scotland. In more than one letter of this early phase he admitted that he was still an "outsider," that his relations with English people did not progress very far; but his imaginative contact with them was fruitful enough, as his later novels and stories with English themes were to show.

REFERENCES

1. *H.J.A.*, pp. 41–2.
2. *H.J.A.*, p. 40.
3. *H.J.A.*, pp. 58–9.
4. *H.J.A.*, p. 373.
5. *H.J.A.*, p. 338.
6. *H.J.A.*, p. 342.
7. *H.J.A.*, p. 22.
8. *H.J.A.*, p. 161.
9. *H.J.A.*, p. 240.
10. *H.J.A.*, pp. 268–9.
11. *H.J.A.*, p. 415
12. Leon Edel, *Henry James: The Untried Years*, 1953, pp. 176–86.
13. *The Notebooks of Henry James*, edd. F. O. Matthiessen and Kenneth B. Murdock, 1947, p. 35.
14. *H.J.A.*, p. 34.
15. *H.J.A.*, pp. 27–8.
16. *H.J.A.*, p. 507.
17. *H.J.A.*, p. 283.
18. *H.J.A.*, p. 509.
19. *Selected Letters of Henry James*, ed. Leon Edel, 1956, pp. 51–2.
20. *L.*, I, pp. 24–5.
21. *H.J.A.*, p. 586.
22. *H.J.A.*, p. 593.

CHAPTER II

THE PASSIONATE PILGRIM AND OTHER AMERICAN THEMES

The most interesting result of his 1869–70 visit to Europe was a group of stories—"A Passionate Pilgrim" (1871), "The Madonna of the Future" (1873), and some that he never reprinted—which owe much of their vitality to the descriptions of places visited by the characters; and also a series of travel sketches of Chester, Lichfield, Warwick, Wells, Salisbury, Venice, Rome, and other places, which began to appear in 1872.

In the opening pages of "A Passionate Pilgrim" the narrator, an American, describes his arrival at "a certain antique hostelry, much to the east of Temple Bar, deep in the quarter that I had inevitably figured as the Johnsonian." Immediately, we find ourselves in the midst of an American's long-cherished, long-foreseen London:

Here, on the first evening of my stay, I descended to the little coffee-room and bespoke my dinner to the genius of 'attendance' in the person of the solitary waiter. No sooner had I crossed the threshold of this retreat than I felt I had cut a golden-ripe crop of English 'impressions.' The coffee-room of the Red Lion, like so many other places and things I was destined to see in the motherland, seemed to have been waiting for long years, with just that sturdy sufferance of time written on its visage, for me to come and extract the romantic essence of it.

The latent preparedness of the American mind even for the most characteristic features of English life was a matter I meanwhile failed to get to the bottom of. The roots of it are indeed so deeply buried in the soil of our early culture that, without some great upheaval of feeling, we are at a loss to say exactly when and where and how it begins.[1]

Here the narrator first sees his unfortunate compatriot, Clement Searle, who has set his heart upon an English inheritance, of which he is to be disappointed. At Hampton Court, which they both happen to visit on the same day, they become acquaintances and fellow tourists. Searle is one of James's recurring American types, the embodiment of hopeless subjugation to Europe. The narrator himself is as far gone as reason permits, but his enamoured and obsessed companion has passed beyond this frontier. When they journey together to Lackley Park, the home of the English Searles, they encounter scenes—an inn, a farm, a village green, a village church and churchyard, all uncannily true to type—which inspire a succession of ecstatic descriptive flourishes. In passages of this kind James enjoys going to extremes. The old woman on the village green is "*the* old woman in person"; the ploughboy whistling on a stile has "the merit of being not only a ploughboy but a Gainsborough."[2] After his unlucky visit to Lackley Park, where he is insulted and repulsed by the owner, it is to Oxford that poor Searle repairs for the final stage of his pilgrimage; and there, overwhelmed by the wonders of the university city and surrounded by the sympathy of all who hear of his story, he dies. It is a sad little tale, but with a humorous flavour in the more documentary passages.

"The Madonna of the Future" is a companion piece to "A Passionate Pilgrim." The setting is in Florence, and the "tourist-narrator," on the evening of his arrival, takes a stroll in the neighbourhood of the Palazzo Vecchio. Here he encounters a stranger who rhapsodises on the glories of Florence and its past, reflecting sadly on the poverty of modern life. Unable at first to place him, the narrator suddenly recognises his note:

The mystery was suddenly solved; my friend was the most characteristic of compatriots. He would *have* to be one of 'us,' of the famished race . . .[3]

Their acquaintance develops, they go together to the great galleries and monuments, which are described effectively, and the narrator learns of his companion's consuming passion, which is to paint a Madonna. To this purpose he has for years been utterly dedicated: all he does is merely preparation for it. The woman singled out for the model is now middle-aged, and the canvas remains untouched. The development of the story to its pathetic end, with the disillusionment and death of Theobald, need not be recapitulated here. In a fuller account of it, James's portrayal of some of the characters —notably Serafina, the model, and Mrs Coventry, an American expatriate hostess—would deserve attention as evidence of his growing mastery of national types. Theobald's pessimistic outburst on the American's relation to culture is worth noting:

'. . . We're the disinherited of Art! We're condemned to be superficial! We're excluded from the magic circle! The soil of American perception is a poor little barren artificial deposit! Yes, we're wedded to imperfection! An American, to excel, has just ten times as much to learn as a European! We lack the deeper sense! We have neither taste nor tact nor force! How *should* we have them? Our crude and garish climate, our silent past, our deafening present, the constant pressure about us of unlovely conditions, are as void of all that nourishes and prompts and inspires the artist as my sad heart is void of bitterness in saying so! We poor aspirants must live in perpetual exile.'[4]

This is in striking contrast to the optimism of James's letter to Perry, and to his own solution, his lifetime of solutions, to the American's problem. Whether he ever had moods in which it seemed as desperate as this would be difficult to say. In his study of Hawthorne he referred to the moral pointed by his great predecessor's delicate achievement: "that the flower of art blooms only where the soil is deep, that it takes a great deal of history to produce a little literature, that it needs a complex social machinery to set a writer in motion."[5]

These stories gain by being read in conjunction with the travel sketches. The American literature of travel, to which Hawthorne and Howells also made important contributions, is a very illustrious tradition with characteristics of its own. The appeal is, in general, to an American audience for whom, it is assumed, Europe is a theme of peculiar interest. The emphasis is on the central, typical things, whether glamorous or homely, and on anything which serves to illustrate general differences between the Old and the New World. The American travel writers make common ground with their readers, giving impressions of just those things that would interest the would-be travellers among them. Thus, in describing St Peter's, James is far from scorning the commonplace question about its size: "The place struck me from the first as the hugest thing conceivable—a real exaltation of one's idea of space."[6] He dwells frequently on the fatal expressiveness of Europe to the American sensibility. To an American, "accustomed to our eternal straight lines and right angles," the streets of Chester present "a perfect feast of crookedness."[7] In several places he says what Hawthorne had said before him, that the English do not appreciate their own country, and that it takes an American to respond fully to it. James is at his best when he writes of the elementary delights of travel: its long-awaited moments or little charming surprises. His account of Wells is enhanced by his confession that, before visiting it, he had no adequate idea of what it could offer: "I can wish the traveller no better fortune than to stroll forth in the early evening with as large a reserve of ignorance as my own, and treat himself to an hour of discoveries."[8] His effort to encompass an experience, to take its measure, leads him sometimes into a lavishly idiosyncratic play of language. But the experience itself is never very far from the simpler pleasures.

He continued to write travel sketches for many years, those collected under the title *A Little Tour in France* (1884) being perhaps the best known. It would be difficult to imagine anything more satisfying of its kind than this little book, so modestly adapted to the needs of uninitiated readers, and so full of graceful and witty description. The English sketches were finally collected in *English Hours* (1905) and the Italian sketches in *Italian Hours* (1909).

James's "sense of place" is one of the most engaging aspects of his art. The expression of it increases in imaginative power in his later novels and stories, though the quantity of topographical description as such decreases. It is characteristic of other American novelists also of this period that they give more value than their English contemporaries to the specific places where events occur. The most amazing example is, of course, Hawthorne's *The Marble Faun*, but Howells's early novels are full of passages which illustrate this point. It was a delightful stroke on James's part to place one of Winterbourne's encounters with Daisy Miller in "that supreme seat of flowering desolation known as the Palace of the Caesars,"[9] where the beauty of a Roman spring and that of his foolish little heroine make a charming composition. The settings for Basil Ransom's meetings with Verena in *The Bostonians*—Harvard, Central Park, Marmion—are beautifully realised, and add their distinctive note to the intimacy of those episodes. The Chester and Paris of Lambert Strether in *The Ambassadors*, the Regent's Park and Venetian palace of Milly in *The Wings of the Dove*, the London square in the London light of Ralph Pendrel in *The Sense of the Past*, all show an even subtler blending of the magic of place with the other factors in the adventure of the central character.

James's work during the eighteen-seventies was remarkable for quantity and variety. His periodical publications in 1875, the peak year, reached a total of over seventy. To stories and book reviews were added not only travel sketches, but also dramatic criticism and art criticism, in which his gifts of eloquent and witty description are very generously displayed. In the 1875–6 period he wrote articles for a New York newspaper on general Parisian topics. The stories and novels of this decade reflect a very rapid mastery of the different settings and environments with which his recent travels had made him acquainted. And they present a considerable variety of types of American in relation with significant aspects of Europe or Europeans.

To say that there was no novel of manners in America, and that James's purpose during these years was to develop it, is as helpful an introductory comment on this period as any, though it does not do him full justice and may lead to critical misunderstandings. Writing to Norton in 1871, he said that American life "would yield its secrets only to a really *grasping* imagination."[10] In an essay on Trollope of twelve years later he praised that novelist's handling of American types, adding that "we have not yet learned to represent our types very finely— are not apparently even very sure what our types are,"[11] but he was too modest. During the period between these two remarks his own contribution to the definition of American types was already quite impressive. Its impressiveness can be better appreciated if certain prejudices and misconceptions are removed. It would be very easy to fall into the error of regarding the "international" situations in his novels as of marginal interest since, of course, they involve only those exceptional people who marry foreigners or develop a hybrid, artificial life by living abroad, or those people whose freedom to travel is evidence of lack of commitments in their own society. Against this it may be claimed that the juxtaposing and comparing of Americans with Europeans was a supremely effective means, first, of discovering what the American types were, and then of presenting them sharply and emphatically. The international story is, among other things, a *technical* device for giving definition and saliency to American manners. In such little studies as "The Pension Beaurepas" (1879), "A Bundle of Letters" (1879) and "The Point of View" (1882), where most of the entertainment lies in the observations of the characters, representing different national and social types, upon each other, the virtue of placing Americans in a cosmopolitan milieu is very apparent. The material itself, in a certain sense, needs this development. Many of the wants, aspirations and illusions of Americans could be regarded as either directly concerned with Europe, or, at least, more likely to find full expression in a European environment. Those Americans, one might argue, who actually married foreigners or who became more European than the Europeans in the matter of artistic connoisseurship, were exemplary figures, instructive "cases," and highly relevant to the study of Americanism. When James brought certain characters to Europe he was giving them their opportunity to be more conspicuously American than they could otherwise have been.

James's works, from this period onwards, are rich in documentary material: he was the most intelligent of observers; but it would be unfortunate if all his American types were scrutinised too narrowly from the standpoint of sociological realism. Sometimes he experimented with situations which, at the time, or so he said later, had not yet taken shape in real life: for example, in "Lady Barbarina" (1884), where the English aristocratic girl marries an American. Some of his characters are figures of legend, like poor Theobald. Some are perhaps idealisations, but it is a word to be used with care. James saw the novelist as a poet, and the task of portraying the American spirit, with all its new energy and mobility, might well inspire the imagination to unusual flights of invention. It would have been strange if national pride, affection, poetic fancy, and sheer delight in creative exploration, had not played their part, along with realistic portrayal and analysis, in the building up of this series of works.

He was a pioneer. He was dealing with themes which had not been treated before, and sometimes the result is artistically imperfect, owing to the intractable or elusive character of the material. But there are brilliant successes. His early triumphs and mistakes help us to appreciate the changes in method of the later period.

"Madame de Mauves" (1874) is perhaps the first story in which he achieved a high level of technique in the management of a situation. The central character, Longmore, is a familiar type—the cultivated, polite New Englander living abroad. Introduced in Paris to a fellow American, a woman unhappily married to a French nobleman, he develops feelings of friendship for her to which she responds with gratitude; but a love affair is outside the tradition within which both of them have grown up. Meanwhile M. de Mauves has reached the opinion that it would be better if his wife took a lover instead of spoiling the atmosphere by steadfastly refusing to accept his infidelities. Longmore receives hints followed by broad assurances from the Mauves family that they would be glad if he provided the solution to their problem, and he is told that this idea has been imparted to Mme de Mauves. Nauseated by their cynicism, Longmore is nevertheless profoundly excited. Though he has "no prevision that he should 'profit,' in the vulgar sense,"[12] he rejoices that circumstances are forcing them nearer to each other. There is considerable art in the skilful contrivance of the series of events which, by acting upon Longmore's emotions, eventually test the limits of his ethos. Just at the point when his platonically ideal feelings have reached their most exalted pitch, an incident occurs which changes them. In his excited mood he walks far into the country, encounters an inn in a rural setting of peculiar charm, has a meal out of doors, and rests in the sun. The things around him "conveyed no strained nor high-pitched message, had little to say about renunciation—nothing at all about spiritual zeal." In his changed mood, he finds himself rebelling against "a lurking principle of sacrifice, sacrifice for sacrifice's sake," in his nature: "To renounce, to renounce again, to renounce for ever, was this all that youth and longing and ardour were meant for?"[13] It is while these thoughts are with him that he sees a young French artist, with a woman who is apparently his wife, but the landlady corrects this assumption. They are obviously very happy, and it seems to Longmore that their happiness sums up all that is simple and satisfying in life.

The outcome of it is a conviction that "the only sound policy in life is to grasp unsparingly at happiness," and with this in mind he calls upon Mme de Mauves. But now he wants more than she can give, and as she delivers her lofty appeal to him not to "disappoint" her, not to be "vulgar" where she had thought him "rare,"[14] it overwhelms him that at that moment she should be so beautiful, while her words convey only denial of what her beauty means to him. Their relationship ends with this scene.

The quality of the story lies in James's device of placing his two Americans in circumstances—"hot-house conditions" they could reasonably be called—which force them to reveal possibilities such as in a milder social climate would never have come to full expression. In him the change is towards greater freedom; but this has the effect of bringing to full revelation qualities in her which mark her as formidable. Her cynical husband's subsequent suicide is the final evidence of her kind of power, but perhaps this stroke on James's part is excessive.

Roderick Hudson (1875), his first important novel, contains at least two major American situations. The first is that of the American artist aware, like the unhappy Theobald, of the limitations of his native environment, who has the opportunity of going to Italy. There was a colony of such people in Rome in the middle of the century. The assumptions on which they built are expressed in a passage in James's biographical study, written many years later, of one of these artists, the sculptor and writer, William Wetmore Story: " 'Art', in the easy view of the age, was to be picked up in the favouring air . . . the air that in all the world differed most from their own."[15] The subject then is the special question of the American artist, and where he can best be trained. It offered opportunities for a more general exploration of America's cultural orientation towards Europe. Roderick might have been a figure rich in documentary significance; but it must be admitted that James made much less of his fictional case than of Story's true one.

There are inherent difficulties in the portrayal of artists as such in fiction. James is second to none in his ability to describe works of art, but he does not describe the positive qualities of Roderick's works quite so effectively as he depicts the deformities of his general character, so that from the beginning we are likely to be less enthusiastic about Roderick than is his friend Rowland Mallet. We are obliged to take his success largely on trust. So little can be shown of the ways of creative genius that when his powers begin to fail him we do not know what has really happened or what moral can be drawn from it. We cannot say what the relationship is between his sufferings as an artist and his perversity as a man. On the important questions raised by his history—namely, whether Rome was from the outset the wrong place for him, and whether his genius really became extinct or was merely undergoing a crisis calling for patience—no light can be thrown. The treatment of Roderick's failure is on a formidable scale, and the book ends with his suicide, but his "case" remains obscure. In writing of Story, on the other hand, James was able to arrive at a significant and ironical solution:

> This truth—to make the matter comfortably clear— is that the "picturesque" subject, for literary art, has by no means all its advantage in the picturesque country; yields its full taste, gives out *all* its inspiration, in other words, in some air unfriendly to the element at large.[16]

Story, in other words, would have been more of an artist in Boston or in London than in Italy, for there "he would have *had* to live with his conception, there being nothing else about him of the same colour or quality." Where he chose to live there was too much, and in this "too much" James recognises the characteristic note of "the amusement of wanton Italy with her victim."

The problem of Roderick is linked with the problem of Rowland, his benefactor, from whose point of view, in a rather general sense, the events of the book are seen. James's analytical study of this civilised young New Englander merits attention, since it is the first notable evidence of his having learnt from the art of George Eliot. *Middlemarch*, with its impressive portraits of Casaubon, Bulstrode, and Lydgate, carefully observed moral types in specific social contexts, had appeared only a year or two before, and James had written an excellent review of it. His historical relation to George Eliot has been discussed in F. R. Leavis's *The Great Tradition*, chiefly with reference to *The Portrait of a Lady*. George Eliot's grasp of those human qualities which owe something to the workings of social and moral tradition was a very desirable equipment for a novelist ambitious to produce pioneer studies in American character and manners.

Rowland's character is drawn very carefully in relation to the facts of his upbringing. His father, a rich man but the stiffest of puritans, has trained him in abstinent habits. He knows, and is "frequently reminded, that a young man is the better for a fixed occupation,"[17] but having money enough he has no wish to make more, and his education has given him spiritual aspirations which business is unlikely to satisfy. His puritan habit of mind keeps him from unqualified indulgence in aesthetic pleasure, and he is too aesthetically sensitive to be attracted to the useful, as understood in his world: "He was an awkward mixture of moral and aesthetic curiosity, and yet he would have made an ineffective reformer and an indifferent artist." It is part of his pathos that he would sometimes have liked to be a vigorous young man of genius without a penny, but, "as it was, he could only buy pictures and not paint them." But Rowland does not associate himself with pathos. Though he feels "the friction of existence" more than is suspected, he assumes that he is one of the privileged. It is a tell-tale detail that the first work by Roderick that attracts him is a statuette of a beautiful youth drinking from a gourd, an emblem of eagerness, appetite, spontaneity: qualities that Rowland notably lacks. He is, in fact, a victim of "Maule's curse," the New England puritan heritage.

James's portrayal of Rowland raises some curious questions. His behaviour has implications which the novelist, surely, intends us to recognise but which are developed less than might have been expected. For example, his adoption of Roderick is an expression not simply of his generosity but of his having nothing to absorb him in his own life. He admits to his cousin's widow, Cecilia, that he is tired of himself and wants to care "with a certain intensity . . . even with a certain passion" for something, but finds it impossible to feel in this way about "a hospital or a dormitory."[18] Cecilia concludes that he wants to fall in love. He was once almost in love with her. In this state of mind he is ripe, one might argue, for some great piece of refined irresponsibility, some act of sublime inter- ference in another person's life. And people who do such things, to continue the argument, deserve to suffer afresh when their schemes go wrong. The grotesquely heaped-up burden of responsibility that Rowland must patiently endure, when Roderick, Mrs Hudson, and Mary Gar- land all look to him for solutions to hopeless problems, might on this interpretation be regarded as no more than retribution. James's handling of Rowland's ordeal pro- vides abundant material for such a view of him, but his emphasis never falls here. Basically, Rowland is always seen as a good and generous character. It is perhaps more outrageous to readers of our century than to those of James's that anyone's life should be such a blank that he can live so completely for someone else. One is re- minded of Miss Compton-Burnett's passages of dialogue on people who "live for others." It is harrowing to see what becomes of Rowland as his position grows more and more unrewarding, and indeed this painful relationship is handled with great power.

The first thing we learn of Rowland, as the novel opens, is that he "accepted the prospect of bachelorhood" when Cecilia married his cousin, but that when Cecilia became a widow he no longer wished to marry her. There is no one, in fact, that he wishes to marry—until he is fully committed to go to Europe with Roderick; and then he develops a strong feeling for Mary Garland, whose inaccessibility becomes complete when Roderick an- nounces his engagement to her. Mary's inconsolable grief after Roderick's death leaves her still inaccessible and Rowland neither challenges this state of affairs nor looks elsewhere. It would seem that he belongs to the category of men for whom the inaccessibility of a woman is a favourable condition for the development of tender senti- ments. At least, James provides evidence for such a view, but no point is made of it. T. S. Eliot says that, with

Rowland, James "commits the cardinal sin of failing to 'detect' one of his own characters."[19] This seems scarcely just, in view of what James actually tells us about Rowland, but the dissatisfaction it expresses is not wholly without cause. What James thinks of Rowland is a question to which no very satisfactory answer is forthcoming. It is distressing that Rowland experiences no moment of revelation about himself. He learns nothing, he does not grow. His New England surface never cracks, and this makes the reader's experience somewhat claustrophobic. If Rowland's case had been allowed a fuller (which would probably have meant a more tragic) development, the effect, paradoxically, might have been more satisfying. "The Beast in the Jungle" (1903), also a study in frustration, ending with an extraordinary opening up of truth for the central character, is in a sense *less* painful to read.

This is not the only case where James's attitude to the characters he has created may raise questions. Edmund Wilson, in his essay on "The Ambiguity of Henry James," deals fully with this problem.

The American (1876–77) justifies its title in having the most obviously recognisable kind of American character-type as the central figure. There is an inevitability about its theme, that of the American man of action, an embodiment of the national virtues—Newman combines success in business with a fine Civil War record—brought into collision with the old European aristocratic order.

Newman is an engaging figure, though his early speeches to Mrs Tristram, the expatriate American woman who is to introduce him to the Bellegardes, contain what some modern readers will see as ominous elements. He wants to marry "as well as you can." If his success is to be perfect, "there must be a lovely being perched on the pile like some shining statue crowning some high monument." He has always felt that "some rare creature all one's own is the best kind of property to hold . . ."[20] But the frank note of worldly acquisitive-ness, combined with connoisseurship—these are recurring American themes in James's novels—does him little harm. There is something attractive in the simple, un-conscious candour with which he expresses values that would be fatal to human relations, were they not combined with his great virtues: honesty, moral and physical robust-ness, a capacity for tenderness and generosity. Mrs Tristram relishes Newman's type, and her oracular, American busybody's idiom sets him off pleasingly: "You're the great Western Barbarian, stepping forth in his innocence and might, gazing a while at this poor corrupt old world and then swooping down on it."[21] She also relishes the old world into which she introduces him: ". . . In France you may never say Nay to your mother, whatever she requires of you. . . . You've simply to obey. The thing has a fine side to it. Madame de Cintré bows her head and folds her wings."[22] Mrs Tristram has not only the practical function in the novel of bringing to-gether the opposites. As an expatriate, with a charac-teristically hybrid outlook, a woman with plenty of leisure and some imagination eager for exercise, she pro-vides an atmosphere in which the sense of situation can be lavishly cultivated.

So far as local colour is concerned the Bellegarde world offers all that the American heart could wish. The family mansion, which "looks as if wicked things had been done in it and might be done again"; Urbain's pro-Bourbon political sentiments; the bizarre conventions of Valentin's duel, with the Catholic-cum-worldly attitude of his seconds; the deadly chill of asceticism in Claire's taking of Carmelite vows: these are among the salient features of the utterly exotic situation in which the hero is in-volved. The formalisms and mysteries of this "grand old *monde*" (to use an expression of the atrocious Mr Flack of *The Reverberator*) are contrasted with Newman's re-laxed tone and off-hand Americanness. Here we have the first example of James's ability to exploit differences of idiom and manner for compositional ends. Newman's confession to Tristram, on their first meeting, of his objectives in Europe, is engaging in its easy independence of any received cultural norm: "I want to let myself, let everything go. I feel coarse and loose and I should like to spend six months as I am now, sitting under a tree and listening to a band."[23] Nothing very specific seems to be threatened in his next sentence: "There's only one thing: I want to hear some first-class music." Newman's ways of speech serve more than one end. In the face of fine Gallic curiosity, his words "It's just the regular treat of being an American citizen . . . That sets a man right up,"[24] are a pleasing affirmation. His reply to a question about his war service is an admirable stroke of propriety: "Yes, but that was not business—in the paying sense. I couldn't afford it often."[25] No one has written better of Newman than Constance Rourke in a chapter devoted to the latter in her *American Humour*. She sees Newman as firmly established in the national tradition of which she is the distinguished historian. The following passage, which she quotes, places him: "He had sat with western humourists in circles around cast-iron stoves and had seen tall stories grow taller without toppling over, and his imagination had learnt the trick of building straight and high."[26]

The chief defect of this novel is the overtreatment of the Bellegarde situation. The story, especially after Newman's disappointment, is too long drawn out. We see far too much of Urbain and his mother, and Mrs Bread's narrative is very tedious. James's criticism of the novel, when he re-read it more than thirty years later, was that he had mistaken the sociology of the situation. The Bellegardes in real life "would positively have jumped" at Newman. The younger James saw his subject in romantic, indeed in "Gothic" terms, so far as the French characters were concerned. And he allowed this aspect of the novel, which grows in portentousness as the history of the Bellegardes is disclosed, to be developed excessively.

Newman is admirable for what he is, but some readers would have wished for a more realistic treatment. James has a splendid passage on the American business-man in an essay written many years later, where he refers also to an important point of American social life: the separation of the man's life from the woman's, owing to the immersion of the former in business:

> ... He is often an obscure, but not less often an epic hero, seamed all over with the wounds of the market and the dangers of the field, launched into action and passion by the immensity and complexity of the general struggle, a boundless ferocity of battle—driven above all by the extraordinary, the unique relation in which he for the most part stands to the life of his lawful, his immitigable womankind, the wives and daughters who float, who splash on the surface and ride the waves, his terrific link with civilization, his social substitutes and representatives, while, like a diver for shipwrecked treasure, he gasps in the depths and breathes through an air-tube.[27]

Unfortunately for this hero, "whose song has still to be sung, and his picture still to be painted," his world of activities is so "special and occult" that a certain training would be necessary for the novelist who hopes to master it: "Those who know it are not the men to paint it; those who might attempt it are not the men who know it." Considering the artistic level at which the life of the business-man has been treated by writers who have attempted it, this is perhaps a fair comment. James did not try to present the business-man at his work; but he portrayed him on vacation, in retirement or in ill-health and defeat. In his sketches of Newport and Saratoga, published as early as 1870 (and happily reprinted in the 1946 edition of *The American Scene*), there are some very acute observations on the business-men and their womenfolk in these holiday resorts. One feature of the American situation is the exploitation of the man by the woman, whose ambition is simply to spend what he earns. Mr Ruck, in James's story "The Pension Beaurepas," is an extreme case of this form of martyrdom. Ill with the strain of business and incapable of enjoying his European visit, this "jaded, faded, absolutely voided man of business," who yet manages to keep alive a wry American humour, is condemned to watch his wife and daughter spending his money, until finally he confronts them with the rude truth that he is ruined and they must return home. The peculiar horror of their family relationship is expressed in dialogue of a pointedness which makes one wonder why James later failed so completely as a dramatist. The Rucks are Edith Wharton's model for the Spragges in *The Custom of the Country*, which deals more overtly and didactically with these problems in American life.

That *The American* should have been followed by *The Europeans* (1878) is a striking manifestation of James's versatility. In general, the main emphasis of this period is on the portrayal of American attitudes in European settings, and the emphasis in his own life is on settlement in a European environment. But in this excellent little novel he turns away from Europe, the theatre of adventurous experiments and extreme situations, and devotes himself to the quiet family life of an old-world Boston household of conservative outlook. The seriousness and inwardness of the Wentworths' way of life are admirably conveyed. The two "Europeans," Felix and his sister, Eugenia—they are cousins of the Wentworths and have returned from Europe—are received into this well-ordered community, and of course they make a difference, and there are occasions for the noting of points of manners. But the contrasts are not very bold. The adjustment of the gaiety and relative freedom of the visitors to the sobriety of the Wentworths is sensitively balanced. A comparison between this novel and *The American* from the point of view of style is instructive. For example, the latter is full of witticisms, such as the description of Tom Tristram: ". . . very sociable, but this was as much a matter of course as for a dipped sponge to expand."[28] The wit of *The Europeans* is more subdued. James is dealing with a different world, in time and place, and uses a different range of idiom. The great merits of this novel, relatively unrecognised mainly because in James there is so much to recognise, are well expounded in F. R. Leavis's *Scrutiny* essay (1948).

REFERENCES

1. *R.*, pp. 301–2.
2. *R.*, p. 327.
3. *R.*, p. 396.
4. *R.*, pp. 397–8.
5. *Hawthorne*, 1879, p. 3.
6. *Italian Hours*, 1909, p. 150.
7. *E.H.*, p. 55.
8. *E.H.*, p. 101.
9. *D.M.*, p. 70.
10. *L.*, I, pp. 30–1.
11. "Anthony Trollope" (1883), in *The House of Fiction*, ed. Leon Edel, 1957, p. 104.
12. *R.*, p. 265.
13. *R.*, p. 268.
14. *R.*, p. 280.
15. *W.W.S.*, I, p. 82.
16. *W.W.S.* II, pp. 225–6.
17. *R.H.*, p. 29.
18. *R.H.*, p. 25.
19. "On Henry James" (1918), in *Q.H.J.*, p. 132.
20. *Am.*, p. 52.
21. *Am.*, p. 49.
22. *Am.*, p. 88.
23. *Am.*, p. 40.
24. *Am.*, p. 105.
25. *Am.*, p. 96.
26. *Am.*, p. 107.
27. "American Letters: The Question of the Opportunities" (1898), in *The American Essays of Henry James,* ed. L. Edel, 1956, p. 202.
28. *Am.*, p. 47.

CHAPTER III

THE AMERICAN GIRL

By way of further contrast, the same year (1878) produced "Daisy Miller," a little masterpiece which achieved
a deserved celebrity. Here James treats his subject with a
perfect appreciation of its points and potentialities, as he
had not succeeded in doing in *Roderick Hudson* or *The
American*.

The obvious way of displaying Daisy's impossible manners was to bring her into collision with traditional society.
To the world of Mrs Costello and Mrs Walker, the American expatriates in Europe, she is simply an embarrassment and a horror. These ladies represent the framework
of possible courses of conduct, of which her every action
is a conscious or unconscious infringement. But the special
art of James's story lies in the presentation of Daisy and
her indiscretions from the viewpoint of the sophisticated,
but sympathetic Winterbourne. He is susceptible, but not
uncritically so. In fact, he is at precisely the right dis-
tance from her. With his rather fastidious sensibility he
is exposed to every excruciating surprise she can inflict;
and the incalculable is the very essence of her behaviour.
But he is intelligent enough to question his own attitudes:
"He felt he had lived in Geneva so long as to have got
muddled; he had lost the right sense for the young American tone."[1] His response to her brings out what it is the
object of the tale to convey: her elusive fineness. The
more elusive the fineness, the greater the odds against its
finding any place at all in any conceivable record of her
aberrations; and the greater the charm when, after all, it
somehow saves her. " 'Common' she might be, as Mrs

Costello had pronounced her; yet what provision was made by that epithet for her queer little native grace?"[2] The effort to encompass the baffling phenomena of Daisy's behaviour provides Winterbourne with plenty of imaginative exercise, and with the play of his mind the story is kept delightfully alive.

Daisy, and the type of American girl she represents, is continually the subject of unanswerable questions. Like her sisters she has always had, she claims, "a good deal of gentleman's society."[3] When pressed concerning the implications of her behaviour, she takes refuge in irrational evasions and sallies, but apparently with no calculated policy of deception. One might ask in vain what Winterbourne or anyone else was to make of the following:

'I do want to say something'—and Winterbourne paused a moment. 'I want to say that your mother tells me she believes you engaged.'

'Well, I guess she does,' said Daisy simply.

The young man began to laugh. 'And does Randolph believe it?' [Randolph is her unbiddable, nine-year-old brother.]

'I guess Randolph doesn't believe anything.' This testimony to Randolph's scepticism excited Winterbourne to further mirth, and he noticed that Giovanelli was coming back to them. Daisy, observing it as well, addressed herself again to her countryman. 'Since you've mentioned it,' she said, 'I *am* engaged.' He looked at her hand—he had stopped laughing. 'You don't believe it!' she added.

He asked himself, and it was for a moment like testing a heart-beat; after which, 'Yes, I believe it!' he said.

'Oh no, you don't,' she answered. 'But *if* you possibly do,' she still more perversely pursued, 'well, I ain't!'[4]

In the Preface to the "Daisy Miller" volume, James quotes the severe comments of a female critic who had accused him of falsifying the type to which his heroine belonged, through yielding to his "incurable prejudice in favour of grace." The real Daisy Millers, she had assured him, were more awful. James's very mild reply is simply that his "typical little figure was of course pure poetry, and had never been anything else." It is an interesting remark from a novelist to whom the word "documentary" was so important, and who, in this piece, shows a nice touch in his sociological detail. The "poetry" consists perhaps in the bringing together of two indubitably real things which in life were more likely to be found apart. Daisy is the product of a dreadful environment, similar to that of Sophy Ruck and Undine Spragge, and her behaviour reflects it. But, with all her absurdity, she has managed to come by some of the famous naturalness and innocence of the American girl. She is somehow not vulgar, and in her wounded independence she has a genuine if childish pathos. If James's friend was right in ruling out such a combination as improbable, surely she was wrong in saying: "But why *waste* your romance?" This is a case in which romance is far from being wasted. In coming to the rescue of the type and doing all that could be done for it, while exposing its defects sufficiently for social criticism's sake, James is giving poetry its place in the portrayal of manners.

James created a delightful series of American heroines, of whom the same kind of thing may be said: that is, they have features that are illustrative of the American social scene, and they reflect the acuteness of his observation, but in the special range of qualities and opportunities with which he endows them they belong to the world of imagination. As a novelist's resource the American girl of the period was a splendid asset, a subject inviting new departures in the art of fiction. There was scope for poetry, drama, comedy, and tragedy in her freedom and naturalness, which made for movement in societies accustomed to the static and for the unpredictable where be-

haviour tended to follow a pattern. She made for novelty
and freshness of situation.

At the expense of chronological order, it will be con-
venient to consider *The Reverberator* (1888) as a companion
piece to "Daisy Miller." Here, too, the point lies in the
success of the heroine, Francie Dosson, in retaining our
sympathy and the hero's, in spite of bracing shocks.

The Dossons, the father and two daughters, belong to the
well-established category of helpless Americans abroad.
Their helplessness manifests itself in extreme dependence
on the vulgarian journalist George Flack, who shows them
round Paris, orders their dinners and is lavishly "treated"
as a matter of course; an arrangement for which they
are touchingly grateful. Francie, the more attractive
daughter, meets Gaston Probert, a gentle, amiable product of the most Gallicised of American expatriate
families, and he falls in love with her. Francie is not quite
so untaught as Daisy, but Gaston's family is difficult to
please. All might have eventually gone well had Francie
not committed the dreadful error of passing on to Flack
the kind of gossipy information he wanted for his paper
The Reverberator about the personal foibles and disgraces
of some of Gaston's French relations by marriage. The
offending article comes to the notice of the Proberts,
and James does not waste his opportunity of depicting
the anguish of a French family assembled to face a
scandal.

Among the things we must "take" in accepting Francie
is the fact that neither she nor any of the Dossons can
fully understand why this newspaper publicity constitutes
such an offence. She is unawakened to such issues, and
bewildered when obliged to face the Proberts. Steering
Francie through such a situation was a greater feat of
virtuosity for James than his handling of Daisy, because
the outcome was to be the saving of the relationship with
Gaston and a happy ending. In exposing her to Flack he
involves her with the worst that vulgarity could do. In

her delicate, absurd way Francie likes Flack, and shares in the family gratitude for his services to them in Paris. It is, in fact, her queer loyalty to him that is the mark of her fineness. The last scene between them, with Francie in pain and Flack at his crudest, incapable of seeing how he has injured her, is a moving exhibition of moderation and unstudied dignity on her part. More than anything else this scene defines her worth. The charm of the portrait throughout lies in the lightness and control with which Francie's little deficiencies and Americanisms are carried, along with, and inseparable from, her beauty. The paragraph in which her appearance is described ends with the words: "She had a weak pipe of a voice and inconceivabilities of ignorance."[5] James was fond of describing his characters' manner of speech: Francie's words are uttered "in her small flat patient voice," or, in a moment of foreboding, "with the sweetest feeblest fatalism." In references to her voice and manner he succeeds in creating the impression of an almost ridiculously unschooled and unformed, yet truly gentle, nature: "She had usually the air of waiting for something, with a pretty listlessness or an amused resignation, while tender shy indefinite little fancies hummed in her brain."[6] Being unformed works touchingly to her advantage: ". . . her pride, what she had of it, lay in an undistributed inert form quite at the bottom of her heart, and she had never yet thought of a dignified theory to cover her want of uppishness."[7]

In these stories, and in others like "An International Episode" (1878–9), which contains the ingenuous and sympathetic Bessie Alden, the American girl is largely a theme for social comedy, though it is a comedy in which serious issues arise. Even the sad ending of "Daisy Miller" does not make its heroine tragic. *The Portrait of a Lady* is on a different level. It is now sufficiently recognised as a tragic novel of the first order; and Isabel Archer is for modern readers one of the most significant and appealing of heroines. Our sense of her importance is enhanced if we consider her as bearing witness to specifically American values, and paying the price for a specifically American type of mistake. Isabel aspires to a life which will transcend, in freedom and range of experience, the life that European young women of her day were brought up to expect. Her whole approach to life raises questions which, in her age, relate to the role of young women everywhere. The story of what happens to her has the scale of interest, the exemplary value, that belong only to figures of the order of Clarissa Harlowe.

James's portrayal of her may be compared, so far as method is concerned, with his portrayal of Rowland Mallet, though it is on a grander scale. In both cases there are introductory paragraphs accounting for points of character in relation to background and environment. For example, we learn that Isabel is the intellectual superior of those among whom she has been brought up, and this helps to explain some crucial weaknesses:

> ... she often surveyed with complacency the field of her own nature; she was in the habit of taking it for granted, on scanty evidence, that she was right ... Her thoughts were a tangle of vague outlines which had never been corrected by the judgment of people speaking with authority ... At moments she discovered that she was grotesquely wrong, and then treated herself to a week of passionate humility. After this she held up her head higher than ever again; for it was of no use, she had an unquenchable desire to think well of herself.[8]

These descriptions of Isabel in her immature days, with her restless curiosity, her idealistic view of the world as "a place of brightness, of free expansion, of irresistible action,"[9] her warm, generous feeling for life and all its possibilities, are very poignant when re-read in the light of her subsequent fate; but it is necessary to emphasise that James is fully explicit about her faults, of which Isabel herself is also well aware:

> It often seemed to her that she thought too much about herself; you could have made her colour, any day in the year, by calling her a rank egoist. She was always planning out her development, desiring her perfection, observing her progress.[10]

She is capable of something near to ungraciousness in her treatment of Lord Warburton and Caspar Goodwood. Her feelings, after she has sent the latter away from her London hotel, are very disturbed and mixed, but it is candidly stated that "the enjoyment she found in the exercise of her power" looms large among them:

> she leaned back, with that low, soft, aspiring murmur with which she often uttered her response to accidents of which the brighter side was not superficially obvious, and yielded to the satisfaction of having refused two ardent suitors in a fortnight . . . she had tasted of the delight, if not of battle, at least of victory . . .[11]

Her pride in her independence shows itself in her lack of distress when her relatives are unhappy about her forthcoming marriage: ". . . she scarcely even regretted it; for it served mainly to throw into higher relief the fact . . . that she married to please herself."[12] If the European *jeune fille* (a type that James portrays in several novels) has grown up in excessive dependence on the judgment of her elders, Isabel has acquired the fault of deferring to them too little. It is a fatal error on her part not to recognise, until it is too late, how very intelligent Ralph Touchett is: more intelligent than Osmond, and especially on the subject of Osmond, whom he sums up to perfection in their notable conversation before her marriage. But if we are to enumerate Isabel's faults we must not forget that poor Ralph is implicated too. Isabel is a romantic: her belief in the romantic possibilities of her freedom, together with an insufficient knowledge of life, are the causes of her terrible mistake. But Ralph, who, among all the characters, is the chief representative of good values and sceptical wisdom, also allows himself to be beguiled by this conception; and, by persuading his father to leave money to her, he digs the pit into which she falls. Ralph's curiosity, his benevolent connoisseurship, is stirred at the thought of "what a young lady does who won't marry Lord Warburton."[13] Her career will clearly be full of interest and, condemned as he is to mere spectatorship of life, he looks forward to seeing it. He tells his father that he would like "to put a little wind in her sails";[14] he would like to "see her going before the breeze": expressions full of the romantic idealistic vagueness which is Isabel's great danger.

James's method in portraying Isabel raises questions which bear upon his later technique. Some tell-tale passages from the early descriptive paragraphs point to the nature of the method and its disadvantages. In one place he says that "her errors and delusions were frequently such as a biographer interested in preserving the dignity of his subject must shrink from specifying";[15] and elsewhere, that his heroine "would be an easy victim of scientific criticism if she were not intended to awaken on the reader's part an impulse more tender and more purely expectant."[16] Here James reveals something of the embarrassment inherent in the position of the novelist who has committed himself to a role akin to that of an omniscient biographer, in an age of dawning psychology and sociology. It is ultimately a heavier commitment than it is good for a novelist to accept. George Eliot sustained this role with great distinction in cases where she concentrated on areas of character which could be given a kind of finality. James was more "modern" than George Eliot, more liable to raise issues which make inconvenient demands; and, as a pioneer in the treatment of American life, he was accepting a burden greater than that of the

novelist who works within an established tradition of
manners and character-types. There is no limit to the
questions a reader may ask of a novelist who, by explain-
ing so much, places himself in the vulnerable position of
being accountable for all. *The Portrait of a Lady*, great
work of art though it is, is faulty in this respect: the mode
of presentation is such as to awaken in the reader a
curiosity which is not fully satisfied. It is about Isabel's
relations with Mme Merle and Osmond that questions
are liable to arise. Is James's portrayal of these characters
such as to explain Isabel's attachment? As soon as we
begin to examine details, we realise that we are up against
complex matters of social and cultural history which it
ought not to be necessary for the reader of a novel to be
concerned with. Ralph describes Osmond as a "sterile
dilettante,"[17] and the words go straight to the mark, yet
Isabel is unshaken. How can we appreciate fully his
power to interest her without more knowledge than James
gives us of his actual tastes, the quality of his comments
on specific works of art, and so forth? But if we had more
detail of this kind, we should also need the corresponding
detail about her: how much did she know, and where was
she liable to be impressed and therefore misled? In the
interests of a completely realistic understanding of the
situation, we should need to know more of the background
of social and moral attitudes against which such a life
as Osmond's would seem "fine."

These questions only occur to us because in the early
part of the book our sympathetic interest has been aroused
to an unusual degree and then frustrated. In some passages, before the Osmond situation begins, we are very
near to Isabel. When the most crucial choice of her life is
about to be made, we feel that we know her less well.
We are not permitted to live through these experiences
with her. James places a serious strain upon us by sharing
with us his "omniscient novelist's" knowledge of Osmond
and Mme Merle as conspirators, so that we know the

kind of trap she is falling into without being near enough
to feel intimately what the situation means to her; and
from the early part of her married life we are excluded
entirely. Later, we again see things from Isabel's standpoint, and in the marvellous forty-second chapter (the
"backward glance") where we are indeed near to her,
much—though not all—is done to make her initial error
imaginatively convincing:

> Ah, she had been immensely under the charm! It had
> not passed away; it was there still: she still knew per-
> fectly what it was that made Osmond delightful when
> he chose to be . . . A certain combination of features
> had touched her, and in them she had seen the most
> striking of figures. That he was poor and lonely and yet
> that somehow he was noble—that was what had inter-
> ested her and seemed to give her her opportunity.
> There had been an indefinable beauty about him—in
> his situation, in his mind, in his face. She had felt at the
> same time that he was helpless and ineffectual, but the
> feeling had taken the form of a tenderness which was
> the very flower of respect . . . And she had loved him,
> she had so anxiously and yet so ardently given herself
> —a good deal for what she had brought him and what
> might enrich the gift. As she looked back at the passion
> of those full weeks she perceived in it a kind of maternal
> strain . . .[18]

The difficulty that still remains is that of appreciating
Osmond's "beautiful mind," and its appeal for her. It is
similar to the difficulty of appreciating Roderick Hudson
as an artist. The life of the artist or the connoisseur of the
arts seems not to lend itself to portrayal by a novelist concerned with matters of value, because the values are so
elusive.

The statement of Isabel's situation in its completed
form (whatever we may think of it in process of forma-
tion) is a great imaginative achievement. The perfect

opposition between the freedom that Isabel had planned
for herself and the servitude into which she is trapped is
an extraordinary revelation of how the innocent can hurt
themselves through mistaking the nature of things. One
of the most poignant passages in the early descriptions of
Isabel tells us that "Deep within her soul—it was the
deepest thing there—lay a belief that if a certain light
should dawn she could give herself completely; but this
image, on the whole, was too formidable to be attractive."[19] And we are reminded of this when Osmond makes
his first declaration. The terrible perfection of her plight
in marriage lies in the fact that, with her capacity for self-
giving, the quality that makes her most deeply and truly
a woman, she cannot wish for her freedom again. Osmond
has drawn out the best in her, though only to trample
upon it.

It was suggested earlier that, with her freedom-loving
aspirations and her confidence in her own power to choose,
Isabel makes a specifically American type of mistake. Is
there any thematic significance (one needs to beware of
the "thematic" in these days) in the fact that her undoing
is brought about by Americans? Isabel has something of
the acquisitiveness characteristic of other American pilgrims in Europe. She desires "experiences." It could be
said that such a programme in life was bound to lead to
disillusion, and that the desiccated sensibility, the root-
lessness and corruption, of an Osmond represent the consequences of a similar programme carried to the furthest
extreme. It appears to be one of the ironies of the novel
that the trap laid for her comparatively innocent irresponsibility should be the work of those in whom the poison
has done its worst. Isabel is a long way from Osmond's life-
killing aestheticism, but the cherishing of ideal conceptions
of life *is* an aestheticism which may lead to sterility.

The Portrait of a Lady is a landmark in James's career,
partly because it is the culmination of a phase, the greatest novel of his early period; and partly because it is his

last major work before his parents died in 1882. His visits to the United States at this time were the last until the momentous tour of 1904–5 to which we owe his greatest travel book *The American Scene*. It is entirely characteristic of the mobility of his imagination that, of his next two novels, *The Bostonians* (1885–86) is his most thorough-going treatment of Americans in America, while the other, *The Princess Casamassima* (also 1885–86), is a pecu-liarly adventurous exploration of rather unexpected areas of English life.

It would be a pleasure to dwell lengthily on *The Bos-tonians*, which F. R. Leavis describes as "a wonderfully rich, intelligent and brilliant book."[20] *The Portrait of a Lady* and it are, for him, "the two most brilliant novels in the language."[21] Such space as can be allotted to it here may most usefully be given to its heroine, Verena Tar-rant, who is not always appreciated at her full value. Of all James's American heroines none is more delightful company; which is perhaps surprising since the company that she has kept all her life is so queer:

> She had been nursed in darkened rooms; she had begun to 'attend lectures,' as she said, when she was quite an infant, because her mother had no one to leave her with at home. She had sat on the knees of somnambulists, and had been passed from hand to hand by trance-speakers; she was familiar with every kind of 'cure', and had grown up among lady-editors of newspapers advocating new religions and people who disapproved of the marriage-tie.[22]

In surrounding her with such people and saddling her with the "little gift" for rhapsodical utterance, James imposes upon himself the kind of handicap which, as we have seen in his treatment of Daisy and Francie, it was his pleasure to overcome. The charm of Verena is that she is so utterly eligible for rescue from the life to which, in her easy good faith, she has committed herself.

Verena's simplicity and good nature, and her complete lack of self-conceit, are evident from the first. Before she makes her speech, in the meeting at Dr Prance's, she appeals to Mrs Farrinder, one of the battle-axes of the feminist movement, for a "lead": "I want a starting-point—I want to know where I am . . . Just two or three of your grand old thoughts."[23] She accepts her charlatan father's manipulations and strokings as necessary for her performance: " 'Well, I can't say much except when father has worked on me,' Verena answered, with an ingenuousness beside which humility would have seemed pretentious."[24] As for accepting Olive Chancellor's invitation to visit her, "she was young enough to enjoy any journey in a horse-car, and she was ever-curious about the world." It is her gentle docility and unwillingness to hurt that keep her loyal for so long to Olive and to the movement, when more natural forces are pulling her away.

There is charming comedy in the situations arising out of her attitude to young men. She is obliged to have an attitude, since there is no likelihood that they will leave her alone. It becomes understood between herself and Olive that young men represent a "phase" for her: "The sooner she got through it the better . . . and she seemed to think that her transit would be materially quickened by a visit to Mr Burrage's rooms."[25] In their struggle against men, "the more they knew about them the better." The difference between her and Olive is engagingly shown in a conversation which follows upon the musical party in Mr Burrage's rooms:

'It would be very nice to do that always—just to take men as they are, and not to have to think about their badness. It would be nice not to have so many questions, but to think they were all comfortably answered, so that one could sit here . . . and listen for ever to Schubert and Mendelssohn. *They* didn't care anything about female suffrage! And I didn't feel the want of a vote today at all, did you?' Verena inquired, ending, as she always ended in these few speculations, with an appeal to Olive.

This young lady thought it necessary to give her a very firm answer. 'I always feel it—everywhere— night and day. I feel it *here*;' and Olive laid her hand solemnly on her heart. 'I feel it as a deep, unforgettable wrong, I feel it as one feels a stain that is on one's honour.'

Verena gave a clear laugh, and after that a soft sigh, and then said, 'Do you know, Olive, I sometimes wonder whether, if it wasn't for you, I should feel it so much.'[26]

Olive, though by no means happy about Verena's inevitable "phase," is sufficiently schooled in the national ethos to appreciate "the consummate innocence of the American girl" in her, and to realise that she "was not in the smallest degree a flirt, that she was only enchantingly and universally genial, that nature had given her a beautiful smile, which fell impartially on every one, man and woman alike."[27] That such a person should be for so long committed to a movement fundamentally anti-male in sentiment is good comedy.

This friendliness of the American girl gives lightness to a novel, enabling the note of pleasure to be sounded where the manners of other communities would have stifled it. There is extraordinary charm in the episode where Basil Ransom first calls on Verena in her Cambridge home, in the radiance of her appearance as she welcomes him, and in her suggestion that they should walk round a little and see Harvard College. Ransom is a Southerner, and therefore in a position to appreciate this New England frankness and "good faith" as a fresh experience. It is typical of James to heighten values by presenting them in terms of their impact upon the sensibility of a stranger.

He notes how her outspokenness does nothing to compromise her modesty:

'The interest you take in me isn't controversial—a bit. It's quite personal'. . . she could speak such words as these without the smallest look of added consciousness coming into her face, with the least supposable intention of coquetry, or any visible purpose of challenging the young man to say more.[28]

She has a vein of American humour, and enjoys his provocations: " 'Why, sir, you ought to take the platform too; we might go round together as poison and antidote'."[29] With her unawareness of the incongruity of her position, and her slowness in recognising her true destiny —that she is made for love—Verena is a delight throughout. If the novel has a flaw it is in the elaborately-staged violence of the ending. One could have wished for less cruelty to Olive.

In this brief survey of novels and stories published between the early eighteen-seventies and the late eighteen-eighties there are many omissions: *Watch and Ward* (1871) and *Confidence* (1879), his weakest novels; *Washington Square* (1880), a New York novel of high quality, with a penetrating study of a father-daughter relationship; and several shorter pieces with inter-cultural situations. An examination of these works, with a much closer perusal of those already discussed here, would yield further variations on the familiar types. There are yet more American girls—Miranda Hope, the rather farcical New England maiden in "A Bundle of Letters"; Aurora Church in "The Pension Beaurepas," whose dreadful Europeanised mother has driven her to desire her own country; and the delightful "Pandora" (1884), the "self-made girl." There are more American business-men, parents, artists, expatriates and passionate pilgrims; and the American child is here and there ominously documented. No inventory such as this can do anything to suggest the quality of James's "notation," the wit and ease and verbal felicity with which points of social manners are presented as part of the total imaginative effect. They are not always singled out for special emphasis and readers, especially non-Americans, may easily underestimate them.

REFERENCES

1. *D.M.*, p. 15.
2. *D.M.*, p. 27.
3. *D.M.*, p. 14.
4. *D.M.*, pp. 72–3.
5. *R.*, pp. 14–15.
6. *R.*, p. 26.
7. *R.*, p. 54.
8. *P.L.*, p. 52.
9. *P.L.*, p. 52.
10. *P.L.*, p. 55.
11. *P.L.*, p. 174.
12. *P.L.*, p. 378.
13. *P.L.*, p. 159.
14. *P.L.*, p. 196.
15. *P.L.*, p. 52.
16. *P.L.*, p. 53.
17. *P.L.*, p. 374.
18. *P.L.*, p. 463.
19. *P.L.*, p. 55.
20. *G.T.*, p. 138.
21. *G.T.*, p. 153.
22. *B.*, p. 82.
23. *B.*, p. 57.
24. *B.*, p. 80.
25. *B.*, p. 136.
26. *B.*, p. 142.
27. *B.*, p. 112.
28. *B.*, p. 209.
29. *B.*, p. 88.

CHAPTER IV

ENGLISH THEMES

In his early sketch of Chester, James wrote of the ways of life expressed by its streets:

> . . . The tone of things is somehow heavier than with us; manners and modes are more absolute and positive; they seem to swarm and to thicken the atmosphere about you. Morally and physiologically it is a denser air than ours. We seem loosely hung together at home, as compared with the English . . .[1]

His sense of the "density" of English social life causes him, in his novels and stories, to treat certain aspects of it—the more typical from his American's point of view—with a peculiar lavishness and thoroughness. Where else would one look for so admirable or so sustained a description of the spectacle of Hyde Park and Rotten Row as in the opening pages of "Lady Barbarina"? It is seen through the eyes of a much travelled, elderly couple "of that nationality for which Hyde Park at the height of the season is most completely illustrative":

> It was all striking, all pictorial, and it made a great composition . . . Certain things were salient, pervasive—the shining flanks of the perfect horses, the twinkle of bits and spurs, the smoothness of fine cloth adjusted to shoulders and limbs, the sheen of hats and boots, the freshness of complexions, the expression of smiling talking faces, the flash and flutter of rapid gallops. Faces were everywhere, and they were the

great effect—above all the fair faces of women on tall
horses, flushed a little under their stiff black hats, with
figures stiffened, in spite of much definition of curve,
by their tight-fitting habits. Their well-seamed helmets,
their neat compact heads, their straight necks, their
firm tailor-made armour, their frequent hardy bloom,
all made them look singularly like amazons about to
ride a charge. The men, with their eyes before them,
with hats of undulating brim, good profiles, high col-
lars, white flowers on their chests, long legs and long
feet, had an air more elaborately decorative, as they
jolted beside the ladies, always out of step. These were
the younger types, for many a saddle sustained a
richer rotundity, and ruddy faces with short white
whiskers or with matronly chins looked down comfortably from an equilibrium that seemed moral as well
as physical. The walkers differed from the riders only
in being on foot and in looking at the riders more than
these looked at them; for they would have done as well
in the saddle and ridden as the others rode. The women
had tight little bonnets and still tighter little knots of
hair; their round chins rested on a close swathing of
lace or in some cases on throttling silver chains and
circlets. They had flat backs and small waists, they
walked slowly, with their elbows out, carrying vast
parasols and turning their heads very little to the right
or the left. They were amazons unmounted, quite
ready to spring into the saddle. There was a great deal
of beauty and a diffused look of happy expansion, all
limited and controlled, which came from clear quiet
eyes and well-cut lips, rims of stout vessels that didn't
overflow and on which syllables were liquid and sen-
tences brief.[2]

There is no clearly-marked beginning to an "English"
phase in James's career as a writer of fiction. After "A
Passionate Pilgrim," the fruit of his first enthusiasm,

several years pass before English themes become important. The Gardencourt opening of *The Portrait of a Lady*, and the study of Lord Warburton, are well-known early examples; and there are longish stories of the same period —"An International Episode," "The Siege of London," and "Lady Barbarina"—dealing with Anglo-American situations, in which English aristocrats and their ways are acutely observed. But James was still occupied also with his Americans in settings other than English: *The Bostonians* and *The Reverberator* were still to appear. In the latter half of this decade, English subjects loom larger, and in the eighteen-nineties they predominate. He developed a connoisseur's interest in the points of the English social saga. One might, for example, make a sizable collection of his pointed allusions to the London "season," and to the Londoner's habit of leaving town at certain times of the year. Setting the scene for a new episode of his story, the narrator of that brilliant *tour de force* "The Coxon Fund" (1894) begins:

> I had almost avoided the general election, but some of its consequences, on my return, had smartly to be faced. The season, in London, began to breathe again and to flap its gilded wings. Confidence, under the new Ministry, was understood to be reviving, and one of its symptoms, in a social body, was a recovery of appetite. People once more fed together . . .[3]

There are numerous references, with the same flavour of the "documentary" and the "illustrative," to the conventions of dining. The stages of the action in many stories of this period are linked with such routines as dressing or assembling for dinner, the question of who goes in with whom being often relevant. We know from his letters what James thought of this way of life. In a letter of 1878 to William he says that the English country house has "at moments, for a cosmopolitanised American, an insuperable flatness." But in the next sentence he admits that, "there is no doubt of its being one of the ripest fruits of time."[4] Writing to Norton in 1886 he describes English upper-class life as "rotten and collapsible," like that of the French *ancien régime*, and "grossly materialistic"; and in the same letter he says: "The gilded bondage of the country house becomes onerous as one grows older, and then the waste of time in vain sitting and strolling about is a gruesome thought in the face of what one wants to do with one's remnant of existence."[5] But he enjoyed his visits to certain houses, and as an artist he responded to the expressiveness of English social forms. On the whole, specific social criticism is not stressed in these stories. Country-house visiting is regarded, in general, as a game which all play who are eligible. But his imaginative treatment of its routines and pastimes is sometimes such as to convey, if only lightly, an element of the grotesque and the unnatural. Animal imagery often occurs: either we are in a world peopled with strange beasts, or there are performances in an arena before beguiled spectators. In "The Two Faces" (1900) the guests at Burbeck are regaled with a very sinister exhibition: the first appearance of the newly-married Lady Gwyther, who has been taken in hand with malignant effectiveness by Mrs Grantham, the jilted mistress of her husband. She has superintended Lady Gwyther's visits to the dressmaker, thus ensuring that this first appearance—from which, of course, one never recovers—will be disastrous. The weekend party is compared to a Roman mob at the circus, assembled "to see the next Christian maiden brought out to the tigers."[6] One of the more appalling of these parties is that in which the novelist Neil Paraday, in "The Death of the Lion" (1894), breathes his last. His predatory hostess is Mrs Weeks Wimbush, "wife of the boundless brewer and proprietress of the universal menagerie"; and in her house, "as everybody knows, on occasions when the crush is great, the animals rub shoulders with the spectators and the lions sit down for whole evenings with the lambs."[7] Mundham in "Broken Wings" (1900) is notable for the congruity of its arrangements: its "Saturday-to-Monday" occasions are described as "great gilded cages as to which care was taken that the birds should be birds of a feather."[8]

There are two of James's stories, among his most penetrating, in which a sense of the limits of this kind of life is expressed with awful emphasis. "The Real Thing" (1893) is a story of an illustrator of magazine fiction who, for a time, adopts as models a middle-aged married couple of distinguished appearance and carriage, who hope they may be of some use for drawings where "the real thing" —that is, real gentility—is needed. "Naturally, it's more for the figure that we thought of going in," Major Monarch explains. "We can still hold ourselves up . . ."[9] Whatever the American male in James's writings was capable of, holding himself up was usually not his strong point. Major Monarch offers proof of his claim:

> I could take his measure at a glance—he was six feet two and a perfect gentleman. It would have paid any club in the process of formation and in want of a stamp to engage him at a salary to stand in the principal window.[10]

These people have lost their money. As the Major admits in a later conversation, they have tried everything, but the market is overcrowded with people of his like ("*Gentlemen*, poor beggars who have drunk their wine, who have kept their hunters!"),[11] ready to take the humblest jobs. With their good manners, their self-control (Mrs Monarch bursts into tears at one point, but quickly dries them), the tact with which they try not to be a nuisance, they *are* the real thing in a sense which commands compassion and a measure of respect. So brief a summary of the story as this cannot do justice to James's sensitive handling of the small points of behaviour and attitude which count in such a portrayal. But how completely and damningly they embody, in their very perfection, the limits of the life which has been their all:

> It was in their faces, the blankness, the deep intellectual repose of the twenty years of country-house visiting which had given them pleasant intonations . . . I could see the rich covers the Major had helped to shoot and the wonderful garments in which, late at night, he had repaired to the smoking room to talk about them. I could imagine their leggings and waterproofs, their knowing tweeds and rugs, their rolls of sticks and cases of tackle and neat umbrellas; and I could evoke the exact appearance of their servants and the compact variety of their luggage on the platforms of country stations.[12]

That they should now be driven by poverty to exploit their only resource, their appearance, for money, is irony enough; but the ultimate point of the story, its final crushing irony, is that they are no good as models, even in illustrations of gentlefolk. At first, the artist admits, with reference to Mrs Monarch:

> . . . I was extremely pleased with her lady-like air, and it was a satisfaction, on coming to follow her lines, to see how good they were and how far they could lead the pencil. But after a little skirmishing I began to find her too unsurmountably stiff; do what I would with it my drawing looked like a photograph or a copy of a photograph. Her figure had no variety of expression— she herself had no sense of variety . . . She was always a lady certainly, and into the bargain was always the same lady. She was the real thing, but always the same thing.[13]

The plebeian Miss Churm is of more value to him as a model, precisely because "she had no positive stamp"; and also because of her "curious and inexplicable talent

for imitation." The artist finds that his work deteriorates
when the Monarchs are his models: they have got him
into a second-rate habit. And it irritates him that they
do not realise the moral of "their fruitless collaboration,
the lesson that, in the deceptive atmosphere of art, even
the highest respectability may fail of being plastic."[14]

The scene of "The Private Life" (1893) is an inn in
Switzerland, but the visitors assembled there are "just the
people whom in London at that time, people tried to
'get' . . ." They habitually frequent the same places, all
"more or less governed by the laws and the language, the
traditions and the shibboleths of the same dense social
state."[15] The story is one of James's fantasies, the non-
realistic element being used to give a bizarre and appalling quality to the distortions and curtailments of their
humanity which people undergo in the cause of social
life. Lord Mellifont, an accomplished exponent of appearances, is discovered to have no existence except when he
can be seen by others, but with what fullness he lives—
socially, that is—when he is "there":

> He directed the conversation by gestures as irresistible
> as they were vague; one felt as if without him it wouldn't
> have had anything to call a tone. This was essentially
> what he contributed to any occasion—what he contri-
> buted above all to English public life. He pervaded it,
> he coloured it, he embellished it, and without him it
> would have lacked, comparatively speaking, a vocabu-
> lary. Certainly it wouldn't have had a style, for a style
> was what it had in having Lord Mellifont. He *was* a
> style.[16]

There is a charming account of Lord Mellifont sketching:

> He had been selecting his point of view—he took poss-
> ession of it with a flourish of the pencil. He leaned
> against a rock; his beautiful little box of water-colours
> reposed on a natural table beside him, a ledge of the
> bank which showed how inveterately nature ministered

to his convenience. He painted while he talked and he talked while he painted; and if the painting was as miscellaneous as the talk, the talk would equally have graced an album. We waited while the exhibition went on, and it seemed indeed as if the conscious profiles of the peaks were interested in his success.[17]

With his shocking knowledge of Lord Mellifont, the narrator reflects on a question which had hitherto caused him puzzled speculation; namely, what kind of reality lay behind his public manifestations:

I had secretly pitied him for the perfection of his performance, had wondered what blank face such a mask had to cover, what was left to him for the immitigable hours in which a man sits down with himself, or, more serious still, with that intenser self, his lawful wife.[18]

But since he is a public figure even to his wife, only the hours when he is alone (so the narrator had concluded) were relevant. No doubt he rested, but what form of rest could repair "such a plenitude of presence"? The "form of rest," he now realises, is that of a temporary cessation of being! James's model for Lord Mellifont was the painter Frederick Leighton.

Claire Vawdrey, in the same story, is a different phenomenon: a creative writer, but so addicted to the routines of society that, in order to enjoy them, he has an *alter ego* who sits in his room writing the works that keep up his fame. James had Browning in mind in creating this figure.

Similar in several respects is *The Sacred Fount* (1901), one of James's richest and most ambitious fantasies, where the setting for the curious phenomena observed (or imagined) by the narrator is a country house where a party assembles for the weekend. It is an essential element in the total effect that the narrator should be continually aware of the points of the social system, and that the guests should be seen, and should see each other, as incessantly engaged in some game which may involve the use of accepted appearances as cover. Routines, or the equally conventional lack of them, provide a kind of pattern of decorum within which the particular manifestations which are of burning interest to the narrator take on a mysteriously formalised quality. If the narrator is right —that is, if Guy Brissenden is really aging while his wife grows younger, and May Server's intelligence is being depleted to provide her lover with unwonted brilliance— then much of this country house behaviour is like an elaborate camouflage for a conspiracy or a secret cult.

The narrator has an unnatural mystery on his mind, but in such places as Newmarch there is always an element of mystery. Love affairs and flirtations are frequent, and anyone may be involved or be thought to be involved. Throughout the novel we see, through his eyes, couple after couple inscrutably communing, the same people paired off in endlessly differing ways; and conversation after conversation takes place in which varying views are put forward of what is really happening. The effect of the narrator's obsession is to give a more lurid colouring or a sharper outline to all this common form of sexual as of social by-play. In some episodes, especially those in which, to the narrator's vision, the plight of the victims is built up to its most portentous proportions, one has a sense of the uncanny possibilities lurking beneath the appearances fostered by a society so schooled. Sometimes the opposite effect, one of anti-climax, is achieved. An atmosphere dense with mystery is broken into by the voice of dull commonplace.

There is no suggestion that the sensitive observer is an American, but his attitudes are in many respects those of a person on the fringe of a society and avidly curious about its ways. No attempt can be made here to solve the problem of the novel's meaning, and it is difficult to make any brief statement about it which does not do an injustice to its queer but entertaining contradictions.

But it may be suggested that one function, among others, of the Sacred Fount theme was to enable James to state, with greater imaginative freedom and zest than elsewhere, how portentous and unnerving English fashionable life could be.

In some stories he makes very effective play with points of contrast between English and American manners. In "Lady Barbarina" the rich young American, Jackson Lemon, is informed, but in the lightest way, that his attentions to Barbarina, daughter of Lord Canterville, have reached certain limits, and that her father will ask him in a day or two what his "intentions" are; but, of course, he will do so with perfect tact. Lemon is rather pained at this departure from American freedom and vagueness: "It's very different in my country. There a man may see much of a girl; he may freely call on her, he may be constantly with her . . ."[19] The complete irrelevance of parents when young people are in love is a familiar theme in American novels of the period. Jackson resolves to act first, and a documentary scene with Barbarina's father follows. Lady Agnes Dormer, in *The Tragic Muse* (1889–90), gives an exemplary exhibition of thwarted maternal hopes in the scene, mercifully not presented directly, in which she scolds her son Nick for forfeiting Mr Carteret's bequest through his failure to marry Julia and his abandonment of a political career. She is the impoverished widow of an important public figure, and intensely frustrated: "Everything's odious, down to living in a hole with one's girls who don't marry . . ."[20] James's English peers and dowagers have all the splendour of their kind. In his portrait of Lady Agnes he succeeds in scaling the steep extremes of the English aristocratic temper without caricature. This novel contains other excellent portraits of English types. Nick's sister Biddy is a well observed example of the sweet English girl, living within the Dormer conventions and limited but not hardened by them. Her conversation with

Peter Sherringham (BK. V, ch xxix), whom she loves, and with whom she keeps up a brave little game of saying what native generosity together with convention prescribe, illustrates her goodness and her limits. That she lacks the untaught graces of some of the American heroines, as well as the inadequacies of others, is a point which must occur to a reader interested in James's work as a whole.

Mr Carteret, the wealthy old parliamentarian who has adopted Nick as his heir, is a masterpiece of clear-cut portraiture. He is a very clear-cut person: even on his death-bed his habits of precision are maintained:

> He had practised lucidity all his life, had expected it of others and had never given his assent to an indistinct proposition.[21]

His response to the news of Nick's engagement to Julia had been characteristic: "That's very suitable. I should think it would answer."[22] Perhaps the following descriptive paragraph does as much as a single quotation can do to illustrate the curious economy of Mr Carteret's mind and manner:

> Nick was always struck with the rare simplicity—it came out in his countenance—of one who had lived so long and seen so much of affairs that draw forth the passions and perversities of men. . . . It was as if experience, though coming to him in abundance, had dealt with him so clean-handedly as to leave no stain, and had moreover never provoked him to any general reflexion. He had never proceeded in any ironic way from the particular to the general; certainly he had never made a reflexion upon anything so unparliamentary as Life. He would have questioned the taste of such an extravagance and if he had encountered it on the part of another have regarded it as an imported foreign toy with the uses of which he was unacquainted.

Life, for him, was a purely practical function, not a question of more or less showy phrasing. It must be added that he had to Nick's perception his variations— his back windows opening into grounds more private. That was visible from the way his eye grew cold and his whole polite face rather austere when he listened to anything he didn't agree with or perhaps even understand; as if his modesty didn't in strictness forbid the suspicion that a thing he didn't understand would have a probability against it. At such times there was something rather deadly in the silence in which he simply waited with a lapse in his face, not helping his interlocutor out.[23]

These qualities—the precision, the dryness of his values; his perfect amenity, within a world of neatly articulated conditions; the quiet authority of his exclusiveness—are a matter of wonder to Nick: but behind Nick's perception is that of the novelist, for whom Mr Carteret is an exotic. His traits of character are all the more firmly and finely incised for being the opposite to what James saw habitually in his American males, with their vagueness of manner, looseness of deportment, shrewd humorous assessment of new phenomena, and generally elastic sense of life.

The same feeling for the exotic type is present in the delightful description of Owen Gereth, as seen through the eyes of Fleda Vetch (*The Spoils of Poynton*, ch. xiii), who for the first time has the opportunity to compare his town with his country appearance:

In the country, heated with the chase and splashed with the mire, he had always much reminded her of a picturesque peasant in national costume. This costume, as Owen wore it, varied from day to day; it was as copious as the wardrobe of an actor; but it never failed of suggestion of the earth and the weather, the hedges and ditches, the beasts and birds. There had

been days when he struck her as all potent nature in one
pair of boots. It didn't make him now another person
that he was delicately dressed, shining and splendid,
that he had a higher hat and light gloves with black
seams and an umbrella as fine as a lance; but it made
him, she soon decided, really handsomer . . .[24]

With his heightened response to the national type James
is able here to add a special vividness and piquancy to
Owen's appeal for Fleda.

James's English characters speak more slang than those
of his fellow novelists of English nationality. Sometimes
perhaps this is overdone, but James saw expressive possibilities in the idiom of the leisured. Owen Gereth's limited
vocabulary and lame attempts at formulation are part of
the helplessness, the "blessed manly weakness," which it
would be "easy and sweet"[25] for Fleda to take care of.
The amiable Sir Claude, in *What Maisie Knew*, provides
the finest examples of patrician incoherence:

'. . . We probably wouldn't give you another governess.
To begin with we shouldn't be able to get one—not
of the only kind that would do. It wouldn't do—the
kind that *would* do,' he queerly enough explained. 'I
mean they wouldn't stay—heigh-ho! We'd do you
ourselves . . .'[26]

James's failure as a dramatist on the London stage in
the early eighteen-nineties was not due to an inability to
write entertaining dialogue with an English note. His
desire to produce something with the quality of a perfect
English comedy of manners was strong, and he may be
said to have realised it in *The Awkward Age* (1899). The
conventions of this remarkable novel are such as to produce the effect of a play perfectly acted. It is as if the
novelist were the producer, with an ideal cast, and each
stage direction interpreted to the last nuance of expressiveness. Such a technique imposes severe restrictions.

The characters' minds are not accessible to us, their actions are limited to what would make stage business, and they express themselves mainly in dialogue, the tone of which is carefully described. Through this medium James does elaborate justice to the conversational tone of the London set of which Mrs Brookenham is the central figure. *The Awkward Age* is a monument to a way of life which perhaps had to be seen from James's special viewpoint to inspire such a concentration of expressive detail.

If the fact of his not belonging fully to English society limited him in certain respects, it had the compensatory advantage of causing him to concentrate more sharply on some features which seemed to him central and typical; points which an English writer might perhaps take for granted or be uncritical about. James had not only his American point of view, but also an American audience. It may be claimed that some aspects of the English scene are more vividly and more intelligently treated by James than by any other writer.

REFERENCES

1. *E.H.*, p. 60.
2. *L.B.*, pp. 8–10.
3. *L.M.*, p. 204.
4. *L.*, I, p. 64.
5. *L.*, I, p. 125.
6. *S.S.*, p. 543.
7. *L.M.*, p. 93.
8. *S.S.*, p. 141,
9. *S.S.*, p. 85.
10. *S.S.*, p. 86.
11. *S.S.*, p. 92.
12. *S.S.*, pp. 88–9.
13. *S.S.*, p. 97.
14. *S.S.*, p. 111.
15. *S.S.*, p. 418.
16. *S.S.*, p. 426.
17. *S.S.*, p. 453.
18. *S.S.*, p. 444.
19. *L.B.*, p. 40.
20. *T.M.*, I, p. 223.
21. *T.M.*, II, p. 145.
22. *T.M.*, I, p. 266.
23. *T.M.*, I, pp. 260–1.
24. *S.P.*, p. 112.
25. *S.P.*, p. 139.
26. *W.M.K.*, p. 223.

CHAPTER V

DEVELOPMENTS IN METHOD

It is interesting that James's first novel with an essentially English setting, *The Princess Casamassima*, is an attempt to penetrate to the life of London's mean streets. His direct knowledge of "the general sordid struggle, the weight of the burden of labour, the ignorance, the misery and the vice"[1] of a great city was perhaps not large. Such as it was, he acquired it mainly, as he admits in his Preface, by walking the London streets during the early period of his residence there. The surprising thing is that he came as near to the world of Gissing as he did.

The novel grew from an idea, that of "some individual sensitive nature or fine mind, some small obscure intelligent creature,"[2] brought up in this environment, with a capacity for appreciating things far beyond his range of social opportunity. The subject was to be the combined effect on his fully awakened consciousness of the two contrasting worlds. This theme, as he outlines it, is moving, and so are some parts of the novel itself, but the total work is not quite satisfying. Two crucial places in the novel may be used to test our sense of the soundness or otherwise of the centre. The first is chapter twenty-one, where the young hero, Hyacinth Robinson, after a stormy session of political argument at the "Sun and Moon" to which he contributes a daring little speech, is immediately whisked away by Muniment and his friends to meet the anarchist leader Hoffendahl. It is in the latter's presence (but the scene is not directly portrayed) that Hyacinth gives his fatal pledge to be ready when called upon to commit a violent crime. The chapter has its background the "deep perpetual groan of London's misery" has been more audible than ever in the previous months; but our question is whether the talk among Hyacinth's associates and what we know of his own mental development up to this point quite prepare us for anything so extreme. Our difficulty may be, as it were, in the vertical or the horizontal plane: either Hyacinth's consciousness (which James used, but not consistently, as his "centre") is not rendered sufficiently intensely and convincingly; or the world of the revolutionaries, if we are judging by the criterion of social realism, is not fully enough treated; or both.

The second crucial episode follows immediately afterwards and occupies chapters twenty-two to twenty-six. Hyacinth has now gone to the opposite extreme, and is having his first taste of the world of wealth and culture as the guest of the Princess at her rented country house, Medley. The Princess, formerly the Christina Light with whom Roderick Hudson became emotionally involved, is an unfortunate blend of caprice and the desire to be serious and to be taken seriously. Since we never quite know how deeply she involves herself either in sex or in revolutionary conspiracy, she remains somewhat mysterious, and in a way that becomes boring for the reader rather than fascinating. She talks too much. James treats the Medley episode fairly fully, even to the length of involving poor Hyacinth in social encounters with rich neighbours, so that all the issues—social, cultural, sexual —that such a relationship could raise for the reader are raised; but with an effect of flatness and unreality rather than of magic, if I have not grossly failed in my reading of the book.

Perhaps the most touching episode is in chapter thirty-five, where Hyacinth tries to get nearer to Paul Muniment and reassures himself that there really is "an immense deal of affection between them." The chapter ends with: "He didn't even observe at that moment that it was preponderantly on his own side." The portrait of Muniment is an impressive achievement, if we regard him simply as an element in Hyacinth's experience—an ambiguous element; but this novel, like *The Portrait of a Lady*, is sufficiently informative in its treatment of special social types to make the reader want more—unless he wants something quite different; that is, a closer registration of the central character's inner experience. Hyacinth's suicide is another of James's uneconomically violent endings. On the one hand, we do not know how far he has really been abandoned by any of his friends: he is overwhelmed by a series of chance appearances. On the other hand, we are not near enough to the centre of him to enter fully into the atmosphere of his vulnerability and despair. Yet the book has some excellent character-studies: Mme Grandoni, with her kindly realism and ironical view of the Princess; the Prince himself, a dull man but not a dull portrait; and also the poor people—Miss Pynsent, Hyacinth's second mother, and her friend and counsellor, Mr Vetch, the shabby-genteel old fiddler.

The Tragic Muse, published three years later, is another novel with themes that lend themselves imperfectly to artistic presentation. But they give occasion for plenty of abstract discussion among the characters, and this has its own interest. For example, Nick Dormer's desire to be a painter, in defiance of all the wishes of his family, is a theme for Gabriel Nash's philosophising; but what is not shown is how good Nick's paintings are, or what the experience of being a creative artist actually means to him. When Nash sees his works Nick asks him: "You think then I *have* a fiddle?" and Nash replies: "A regular Stradivarius!"[3] and it is from such passages that we must learn that he is a genuine artist. James's descriptions of Nick's paintings are probably as good as any other novelist could have produced, but Nick remains rather a lightweight character, and no compelling point is made about the mighty claims of the arts in relation to the more external and obvious claims of the community. We sympathise with the needs of his temperament, and applaud his honesty and gentleness, but that is all. The most dynamic figure in the book is the actress, Miriam Rooth, whose rise from obscurity to celebrity is presented with great exuberance. Here James's convictions about the trials and rigours of the artist's life, and also its healthy and joyous aspects—Miriam is full of energy and outgoing good nature—are strikingly illustrated. But the old objection raises its head again. Miriam is a genius, and the problems of fictitious geniuses are all too easily solved. James was the best of dramatic critics and, unlike many dramatic critics, he described the performances of actors. His account of Salvini's Othello (reprinted in *The Scenic Art*) is quite outstanding among descriptions of this kind that I have read. He caught something of the atmosphere of Miriam's success, but his statement of it tends to be merely in eloquent general terms. We are told that "she was now the finished statue lifted from the ground to the pedestal," and that it was "as if the sun of her talent had risen above the hills . . . ,"[4] but we do not quite know how she has arrived or, in any very specific sense, where. Off the stage she is vitally realised but, like the Princess Casamassima, perhaps she talks too much. So does Nash, who seems to combine an element of Oscar Wilde with something of the New England sage: he has been identified with Henry James senior! His mixture of levity and a rather unwieldy wisdom is not always felicitous. But, in spite of these limitations, *The Tragic Muse* is a very successful novel. The English character-types, as we have seen, are richly "illustrative"; and if the artist theme is open to criticism, there is something engaging in the lively conviction and optimism with which the subject is treated by those most concerned.

These large-scale novels of the eighteen-eighties illustrate James's readiness to experiment again and again with new and specialised social phenomena, sometimes at the cost of imperfection in treatment. His later technique was to involve a happier definition of his commitment, so that the proposed subject received a treatment more appropriate to its needs and possibilities. The increased use of the "point of view" meant a less direct portraiture of society, the aspects portrayed being part of the central character's vision. This allows for a limiting and also a heightening: the novelist is on firmer ground. There is also a departure from what may be called the moral historian's approach to character, the approach exemplified in the portraits of Rowland Mallet and Isabel Archer. A character becomes known to us now either through our participation in his imaginative experience, if his consciousness is selected as central, or as he enters into the experience of the person whose consciousness provides the main subject. Characterisation becomes a more purely imaginative achievement: the form and tone of the presentation prevent the wrong issues from arising in the reader's mind.

What is interesting, and not sufficiently stressed, is that James retained the earlier methods—those of the "solid" Victorian novel—until a relatively late stage of his career. If we are looking for examples of his more finished method in this period we shall find them in shorter works: in "The Aspern Papers" (1888), with its admirably controlled single situation, perfectly enclosed within the narrator's point of view, and the masterly distribution of effect at the end over its three culminating scenes; in "The Lesson of the Master" and "The Liar," brilliant stories of the same year.

The Bostonians and *The Princess Casamassima* were unsuccessful with the public, and James began to realise with dismay that he was an unwanted author. In a letter of 1888 to Howells he complained that the demand for his works had been reduced "to zero."[5] When *The Tragic Muse* was no more successful commercially than its predecessors he embarked upon the phase of his career which, from every point of view, was the least satisfactory: his attempt to capture the London stage. His failure is not easy to account for precisely. He claimed to have mastered the whole doctrine and discipline of the French theatre, of which he was a keen devotee. His adaptation of "Daisy Miller" (never performed) and the dramatic version of *The American*, which had a modest run, show that he could make concessions to popular taste. But *Guy Domville* (1895) is merely insipid and ineffective, as far from the true Jamesian note in the novels as from Pinero and Henry Arthur Jones. The terrible occasion on which he found himself on the stage facing the animal noises of an irreverent audience at St James's Theatre was the worst moment of his literary life.

Not being appreciated as a novelist was bad enough; but during these years he was hoping for success with plays that did not deserve it. His *malaise* expressed itself in a group of short stories with tell-tale themes, such as "The Death of the Lion" (1894), "The Middle Years" (1895) and "The Next Time" (1895), whose heroes are sensitive and vulnerable writers, whom the brute public ignore or crudely lionise: "supersubtle fry," as he labels them in a Preface defending the type. They tend to lack every kind of robustness, and are usually not long for this world; in other words, they are not so very like James himself, though sometimes their utterances express elements of his own artistic faith. They represent a side of him which suffered frustration, especially during this period. The stories, though of high quality, may have done his reputation some harm. These delicate geniuses, with their exquisite style and morbid sensibility, are unfortunately too near to the archetypal aesthete and decadent whom it is customary now to regard with disfavour. Paradoxically, it may be said that James could portray such situations with all the more animus and virtuosity for being able, in his happier phases, to be such a different person himself.

It is pleasant to glance at two of his personal relation-
ships during the time when he was suffering these setbacks.
The James of the early London years was a diner-out,
a guest at distinguished houses, but somewhat lonely,
as, of course, his work compelled him to be. Gradually he
began to loom larger in the lives of other people, and his
capacity for friendship and general sociability became
more manifest. Janet Adam Smith's introduction to
Henry James and Robert Louis Stevenson gives an excellent
account of a relationship to which James's contribution
was all sympathy and benign humour. They met in 1885
and saw each other no more after Stevenson's departure
in 1887, but they kept up a warm correspondence until
Stevenson's death in 1894. James was the better friend as
well as the better writer. No one is obliged to like a
friend's work, but Stevenson's foolish and offensive comment on *The Portrait of a Lady*—"Infra, sir; below you"[6]
—is in marked contrast to the generous and charmingly
written account of *Treasure Island* and *Kidnapped* which
James was composing, and which Stevenson saw, at
about the same time. James had an unequalled gift for
saying delightful things about other people's work. "The
said *Catriona* so reeks and hums with genius," he wrote
immediately after that novel's appearance, "that there is
no refuge for the desperate reader but in straightforward
prostration . . . there is a modesty in easy triumph which
your flushed muse perhaps a little neglects."[7] He criticises
too, but in a manner so tempered by admiration and
respect that there is not a word which could not be read
with pleasure by the recipient. James's epistolary style
had now reached a florid stage, and was to develop towards even greater exuberance: "Roast yourself, I be-
seech you, on the sharp spit of perfection," he writes in
one of his letters to Stevenson, "that you may give out
your aromas and essences!"[8] Imagery and its "function"
are so much a matter for solemn academic consideration today that it ought perhaps to be stressed that

James, in his letters and elsewhere, habitually used it in play.

The second friendship, beginning in 1891, was with Elizabeth Robins, the American actress and pioneer for Ibsen, who appeared as Mme de Cintré in *The American*. His letters to her, and her reminiscences of their collaboration in theatrical ventures, published in *Theatre and Friendship*, make delightful reading. James was not temperamentally an Ibsenite, but he responded to the challenge of a distinction immensely superior to anything that contemporary English drama had to offer, and he contributed some notices of inimitable flavour to the cause. One of Elizabeth Robins's best anecdotes relates to rehearsals for *The American*, during which James became both curious and anxious to know when actors had time to eat. Finally, he organised refreshments himself:

Somewhere, off-stage, there used to appear a large hamper of delicacies, to which with some ceremony Mr. James would conduct us in two's or three's, as we happened also to be 'off'. He himself, sandwich in hand, would return to the fray with obvious relief and satisfaction . . .[9]

The failure of *Guy Domville* was a fortunate crisis in that it led to a renewal of his aspirations and powers as a novelist; and in the period that followed his methods reached their final maturity. He did not in every case adopt the principle of the point of view. *The Awkward Age*, as we have seen, is based on an entirely different technique, and *The Other House* (1896) is similar. It is typical of James that he should be approaching the problems of the novel from two opposite viewpoints during the same period of his development.

The Spoils of Poynton is an instructive example of the difference achieved when the subject of a story is seen to lie in "somebody's excited and concentrated feeling about something."[10] The dinner-table anecdote that was to provide the "germ" for his novel began with a quarrel between a mother and a son; but as the theme developed in his imagination it took shape as the experience of a third person, a girl, whose relationship with both parties gave her not only a useful point of view as a witness of the situation, but also an intense emotional participation in it. It is important that the heroine should have intelligence and sensibility, compared with the other characters: it is what she sees in the situation, and also what she contributes to it, that determine its value. In principle, this may not seem to be a very significant advance on the technique of quite early works. "Madame de Mauves" is Longmore's story, one might argue, in much the same way as *The Spoils of Poynton* is Fleda's. The difference lies in the greater degree of intimacy with which the events and characters in the latter are shown as, and only as, they affect the heroine. Much more depends on the special interest that her emotional and imaginative response give to them.

She is confronted with a series of very intricate moral problems, which cannot be appreciated unless they are seen also as emotional problems. That is, the point of principle which guides Fleda cannot be safely isolated from its context and considered abstractly, though this is frequently done. Adopting this moralising and simplifying approach, readers sometimes say that Fleda's excessively exalted respect for the formality of Owen's engagement to the hateful Mona is responsible for her failure to make the obvious response to him which would have led to their happiness; but it is not quite in these terms that the situation is presented in the novel. Fleda's desire to be "right" herself, and her desire for Owen's rightness, are inseparable from her tender love for him. It is an aspect of her love that it heightens her sense of pride in high standards of behaviour. It is true that an element of "aestheticism" is present in her—she shares n some measure Mrs Gereth's addiction to beautiful "things," and believes that actions should not be less comely; but if we isolate this factor from her affection the proportions are falsified. And there are other reasons for her insistence on Owen's obtaining formal release from Mona. Owen is fatally attractive to women, and he is weak. What seems a rather perverse fellow-feeling for Mona at this point is perhaps a confused defensive reaction on behalf of herself and her sex. It is not easy to draw an objective moral from this novel, and James has not given us the data for it. Owen's quick capitulation and speedy marriage with Mona are mainly the result of the most wretched of coincidences: Mrs Gereth's sending back of the "spoils." We know nothing in detail of how he behaved at this moment when Mona's grasp strengthens. How sure could one be of Owen in any circumstances? But if we care to indulge in speculative moralising beyond the limits set by the novel, there seems to be no good reason why poor Owen should not be regarded as the fool of the piece, with his mother as a close second.

Most wrong views of James are the result of insufficient attachment to his text, and to the habit of abstracting from it themes and morals instead of responding to its tone. The tone of *The Spoils of Poynton* is the tone of Fleda's emotional and imaginative life, and it can only be caught by attention to the language. Some of the best examples are in the ninth chapter, where Fleda is left to cherish the discovery, which must nevertheless be guarded as a secret, that she is an object of desire to Owen. It was an indiscretion on Owen's part to show it, but she cherishes this too and protects it:

Their protected error (for she indulged a fancy that it was hers too) was like some dangerous, lovely, living thing that she had caught and could keep—keep vivid and helpless in the cage of her own passion and look at and talk to all day long. She had got it well locked up there by the time that from an upper window she saw Mrs. Gereth again in the garden.[11]

But this is not among the best of the later novels. Its ingenuity of structure, though often admirable, is developed to an excessive tightness, and the timing is too cruel. The next work, *What Maisie Knew*, leaves nothing to be desired. It is the perfect example of method as the liberating factor, the means of placing the novelist on the happiest terms with his subject. It is appropriate that its Preface should be the most inspired of the whole series.

Part of the charm and the irony of this novel lies in the fact that the little girl's experiences are seen largely as comedy. Maisie's story, against all expectation (given the world of aberrant adults in which she has been so absurdly condemned to live) is essentially a happy one. This is partly a matter of felicitous plotting. Events so fall out that Maisie, who is increasingly neglected by her divorced parents, is the innocent means of bringing the step-parents illicitly together, and so enjoys, though precariously, a special measure of importance and attention. There is comedy in her being able, with her child's view of things, to thrive imaginatively and morally on varieties of relationship which to an adult intelligence signify disorder. Her capacity to see a fairy-tale quality in these sorry situations reduces their evil to impotence so far as she is concerned. We do not see Maisie as badly hurt; her goodness, together with her lack of specific knowledge, saves situations for herself, and also for us, so that her ardent misconceptions give us nothing but delight. There is comedy in the safe limits of her awareness, within which she and her depraved elders and the reader are spared so much, but also in the fact that, within these limits, the grotesqueness of her elders is as much exposed as it is. The unimportance of her father and mother when Maisie is not observing them is part of what the form of the novel implies. It is a stroke of satire to have made them of interest only when thus caught in the fact of their abysmal parental baseness; and the interest of this lies mainly in what her tender fancy makes of it.

The little girl is, of course, completely serious; she is unconscious of comic implications; and as the narrator's consideration for her and her point of view is always central, a certain adjustment of style is involved in the development of so sophisticated a treatment. In approaching the technique of presentation we have James's Preface to build upon. Maisie's situation is shown, he writes, "only through the occasions and connexions of her proximity and her attention; only as it might pass before her and appeal to her, as it might touch her and affect her, for better or worse, for perceptive gain or loss . . ." But although it is seen largely in terms of images and notions drawn from her own repertory of experience, something is added: ". . . our own commentary constantly attends and amplifies." It is Maisie's relation to "the facts of her spectacle," "her activity of spirit, that determines all our own concern—we simply take advantage of these things better than she herself."[12] Of these two factors, the contribution made by Maisie is the main subject of the Preface, and is described in words which convey the joy of a fulfilled artist:

> . . . she has the wonderful importance of shedding a light far beyond any reach of her comprehension; of lending to poorer persons and things, by the mere fact of their being involved with her and by the special scale she creates for them, a precious element of dignity. I lose myself, truly, in appreciation of my theme in noting what she does by her 'freshness' for appearances in themselves vulgar and empty enough. They become, as she deals with them, the stuff of poetry and tragedy and art . . .[13]

The novel is, in this sense, Maisie's: she "gives" us its incomparable scenes: ". . . she treats her friends to the

F   H.J.

rich little spectacle of objects embalmed in her wonder."
The Preface has less to say of the delicate role of the
novelist who "gives" us Maisie. One of the effects of his
tone is to preserve distances. His play of mind, his wit, are
controlled and managed with the tenderest regard for
the freshness of her young vision. It is a tenderness which
operates best by not obtruding itself as such. When occasions occur for Maisie to sound her note, his manner is
such as to enable it to be clearly heard without forcing.
His way of appropriating her imaginative world, preserving its freshness, yet bearing lightly on the "actual
facts" of her consciousness, is the very perfection of
tact.

The contrast between Maisie's simple seriousness and
the virtuosity of her creator is most fruitful, because it
is entirely in her interest that his powers are exercised.
Even among James's novels *What Maisie Knew* is remarkable for its contrived felicities, and our pleasure in the
brilliantly designed episodes is all the greater in that their
function is to afford maximum scope for her life-giving
response. The whole ingenious structure is at once a display of wit and an expression of love.

Some of the best passages are those where Maisie's
misconceptions have that element of disconcerting truth
which serves to expose the falsities of her elders. Her
realisation that her mother needs to be loved has the
most subversive results. The Captain with whom she
converses in the park kindles this thought in her by his
praises of her mother. Treating her as a child, he gets
more than he has bargained for: "Say you love her, Mr.
Captain; say it, say it,"[14] she implores him. She pleads
with him not to do it "for just a little . . . like all the
others." "Do it always!" are her parting words to the
discomfited gallant. In her next meeting with her mother,
who begins with a bout of self-pity and self-justification,
Maisie tries to comfort her by saying that the Captain had
also said of her what she now says of herself—that she is

"so good"[15]—and she goes on, in the teeth of her mother's rage and dismay, to confess the timid hope that it might have been with the Captain (now "the biggest cad in London") that she was going away. Maisie's affectionate thought throws her unworthy parent into complete confusion, and so brings out more of the monster in her.

These scenes are essentially comic. Although Maisie sheds tears and has moments of pain and indignation, the extremely episodic character of her relations with her mother—of her whole existence, in fact—limits the scale of the emotional crises. After this scene with her mother, their last, Maisie sits brooding for a short time, but soon she is with the comfortable Sir Claude and life opens up new vistas. The passage of greatest tension in the book is towards the end, where Maisie and Sir Claude have their little jaunt in Boulogne and face the issue of separation. It is an exquisite episode. Certainly there is pain for both of them, and stretches of weary silence; but Maisie has the healthy child's capacity to suffer for a while and then recover. Sir Claude is much the more disorganised of the two. The fact that his inability to part with his mistress, Mrs Beale, is the whole reason for their trouble gives the situation an element of absurdity, in the face of which there is an indescribably quaint and incongruous charm in his relationship with Maisie. When the moment comes for her departure with the faithful Mrs Wix she is ready, and the avoidance of unnecessary pathos gives an absolute rightness to the ending. The wild display of idiosyncrasy on the part of the adults, in the scene before she goes, is in contrast to Maisie's sensible acceptance of things. With Mrs Beale's paroxysms of invective and violence at the triumph of Mrs Wix, the comedy turns purple and rises to melodrama.

One of James's characteristic devices in this late period was to choose fantastic subjects, involving either a complete departure from literal possibility or a bold distortion or simplification. Like Hawthorne, to whom he owed much, he was able through this means to make imaginative statements of great power and subtlety. Such themes also provided opportunities for virtuosity in the writing itself. "The Beast in the Jungle" (1903), one of his greatest short stories, is remarkable for the intensity with which every implication of its subject is gathered up and driven home in the tremendous last scene. The theme is an obsession which entirely dominates the life of the central character, John Marcher: his sense, "the deepest thing within him," that he is being "kept for something rare and strange, possibly prodigious and terrible,"[16] which must inescapably befall him: "Something or other lay in wait for him, amid the twists and the turns of the months and the years, like a crouching Beast in the Jungle."[17] Marcher confides his secret to a woman, May Bartram, whose participation in his curiosity and suspense is the basis of a long friendship. Finally, she makes the mysterious announcement that she has discovered what is to happen to him, but she cannot tell him. As her death approaches he has a distressing and perplexing conversation with her during which, pale and ill as she is, she tries to convey without words the meaning that he is incapable of recognising; and then in despair tells him that what was to happen has happened. Long after her death he has his moment of revelation. It comes to him near her grave in the cemetery which Marcher, now a man without purpose, has formed the habit of visiting with an obscure sense of drawing near to the only thing that has ever given meaning to his life: that is, the old, cherished obsession shared with her. He sees the face of a mourner, a face "with an expression like the cut of a blade," and its effect on him, as he takes in its significance for the mourner and for himself, is that of a death-blow:

The stranger passed, but the raw glare of his grief remained, making our friend wonder in pity what wrong, what wound it expressed, what injury not to be healed. What had the man *had*, to make him by the loss of it so bleed and yet live?

Something—and this reached him with a pang—that *he*, John Marcher, hadn't; the proof of which was precisely John Marcher's arid end. No passion had ever touched him, for this was what passion meant; he had survived and maundered and pined, but where had been *his* deep ravage? . . . He had seen outside of his life, not learned it within, the way a woman was mourned when she had been loved for herself: such was the force of his conviction of the meaning of the stranger's face, which still flared for him as a smoky torch. It hadn't come to him, the knowledge, on the wings of experience; it had brushed him, jostled him, upset him, with the disrespect of chance, the insolence of accident. Now that the illumination had begun, however, it blazed to the zenith, and what he presently stood there gazing at was the sounded void of his life. He gazed, he drew breath, in pain; he turned in his dismay, and, turning, he had before him in sharper incision than ever the open page of his story. The name on the table smote him as the passage of his neighbour had done, and what it said to him, full in the face, was that *she* was what he had missed. This was the awful thought, the answer to all the past, the vision at the dread clearness of which he turned as cold as the stone beneath him. Everything fell together, confessed, explained, overwhelmed; leaving him most of all stupefied at the blindness he had cherished. The fate he had been marked for he had met with a vengeance—he had emptied the cup to the lees; he had been the man of his time, *the* man, to whom nothing on earth was to have happened.[18]

ohn Marcher's "case" might illustrate a number of psychological phenomena which could have been presented with an attempt at straight realism, and indeed

there are passages in James's story where the psychological notation is of the finest. Marcher's prodigious
egoism manifests itself in some very discreet, civilised
ways. One might perhaps claim a religious background
for his obsession: he has the sense of being "called," and
this separates him horrifically from people of common
fate. Some kind of psychic impotence seems to be involved. The advantage of this imaginative device is that
it transcends the limitations of an explicit psychological
or moralising interpretation of character.

REFERENCES

1. *P.C.*, p. ix.
2. *P.C.*, p. viii.
3. *T.M.*, II, p. 24.
4. *T.M.*, I, p. 298.
5. *L.*, I, p. 136.
6. *Henry James and Robert Louis Stevenson*, 1948, p. 166.
7. *L.*, I, p. 213.
8. *L.*, I, p. 163.
9. *Theatre and Friendship*, 1932, pp. 50–1.
10. *S.P.*, p. xiv.
11. *S.P.*, p. 87.
12. *W.M.K.*, pp. xi–xii.
13. *W.M.K.*, pp. xii–xiii.
14. *W.M.K.*, p. 110.
15. *W.M.K.*, p. 154.
16. *Fourteen Stories by Henry James*, selected by David Garnett, 1948, p. 390.
17. *Op. cit.*, p. 396.
18. *Op. cit.*, pp. 431–2.

CHAPTER VI

THE LATE PHASE

In 1898 James gave up his London flat, and settled in an eighteenth-century house in Rye, Sussex. The purchase of Lamb House was one of the landmarks of his life. On the one hand it was a retreat from the consequences of his inveterate sociability in hospitable London: it enabled him to concentrate on the greatest works of his career. But it also enabled him to be sociable in a more distinguished and personal way. Edmund Gosse, A. C. Benson, and others have described the expansive host who greeted them on their arrival at Rye railway station. But James retained his membership of a London club, so he was not totally severed from his former way of life. His characteristically amiable relationship with Rye and its people is described in F. W. Dupee's chapter, "The Lion of Lamb House," in his book in the American Men of Letters series, which provides a rich assemblage of impressions of James's culminating phase.

In the three novels which are usually regarded as the summit of his achievement—*The Ambassadors* (1903), *The Wings of the Dove* (1902), and *The Golden Bowl* (1904), to place them in order of composition—he returned to his early theme of the American in Europe, and one of the minor pleasures of reading these books is that of seeing the familiar points of the saga recurring in more refined or somewhat disguised forms. Strether is yet another passionate pilgrim: his susceptibility to Europe does not fall short of the tradition, of which he is indeed the finest flower; but his response to places as such is only an aspect of his absorbing imaginative adventure.

The Ambassadors is very much a novel of manners: Strether is acutely aware of differences in this respect between Americans and Europeans, and between Americans and Americans, but his reflexions on them partake so much of the peculiar atmosphere of his beguilement that their documentary implications could easily be missed. It is not James's intention that they should obtrude. Similarly, Milly's impressions of the English type, on her first meeting with Lord Mark and Kate Croy at Lancaster Gate, are pleasingly consistent with what we should expect from James's earlier writings which record the American response to England; but Milly is represented as feeling her way, tentatively responding to several things at once, and these perceptions are only part of a total experience of fascinating newness.

What is the subject of *The Ambassadors*? In the first place, it may be said that Strether's adventure taken as a whole is the subject, and this includes a great deal. But central to Strether's adventure is a quest: he goes through several stages of mystification and enlightenment, until finally he reaches the heart of a situation which it was his initial object to investigate. This situation is the relationship between Chad and Mme de Vionnet. In Strether's experience of it we have a perfectly rounded subject: not the whole of the novel, of course, but something central enough to suffice for this brief introductory account of it.

It turns out to be one of the especially typical themes of French fiction: that of a woman ravaged by love for a man younger than herself who is gradually freeing himself from her. The French novelists have excelled in studies of the sufferings of lovers, and here James takes a leaf out of their book: but he presents the theme from a new angle. We approach it through the consciousness of an elderly, somewhat uninitiated but sensitive New Englander, who comes to Paris charged with the mission of rescuing the young man from whatever influences are keeping him away from his father's business. Strether as the centre of consciousness is the perfect choice, because there is no aspect of the affair which is not new to him. He must discover everything for himself. In one sense, of course, he is the least qualified person to take the measure of the situation—he is a disastrous failure as an ambassador, and reinforcements have to be despatched—but his peculiar susceptibility to the charm of appearances has the value of giving freshness and saliency to a theme which, in a world where everyone knows all the answers, can easily become stale.

It was part of the French tradition that a liaison with a gracious and sophisticated married woman could do much for a young lover's manners. Strether has nothing but the Woollett conception of an irregular life to go by, and it is a new thing for him to see what Mme de Vionnet has done for Chad. He had known Chad in his earlier, cruder days, and is immensely impressed by the change, but cannot place the phenomenon for what it is. When someone lies to him about the precise nature of their relationship, he very readily loses himself in a kind of romantic exaltation about it. He falls under the spell of Mme de Vionnet, and his whole conception of the good life is transformed by the graceful values she seems to embody, compared with the provincialism and moral flatness of Woollett. There is something in the bearing of men towards women, and women towards men in this world—Strether often hovers on the brink of interesting sociological discriminations—which compares most favourably with the relations between the sexes in America, where men, in their obsession with business, accept a position of social and cultural inferiority to their rather formidable womenfolk. Under the spell of his illusion he befriends Mme de Vionnet, and fatally jeopardises his relations with Woollett.

James's art is at its height in the *dénouement*, which begins with Strether's little excursion into the country. It is a masterly stroke of irony that he should be going in search of something French, some quintessentially French scene, to satisfy a desire awakened by a Lambinet landscape which years before he had wanted to buy. He finds what he has been looking for: it is almost as if the long-remembered picture had come to life again:

> The oblong gilt frame disposed its enclosing lines; the poplars and willows, the reeds and river—a river of which he didn't know, and didn't want to know, the name—fell into a composition, full of felicity, within them . . .[1]

The whole of this descriptive passage needs to be appreciated along with James's travel sketches, all so illustrative of the old familiar truth that it takes an American to appreciate these things to the full. Strether sees a boat on the river, and this seems again to fit in perfectly with the idea he had set out with:

> What he saw was exactly the right thing—a boat advancing round the bend and containing a man who held the paddles and a lady, at the stern, with a pink parasol. It was suddenly as if these figures, or something like them, had been wanted in the picture, had been wanted more or less all day, and had now drifted into sight, with the slow current, on purpose to fill up the measure.[2]

They do fill up the measure, until Strether's cup overflows, but not with the blissful contentment he has enjoyed up to this point. From the moment when he recognises Chad and Mme de Vionnet, and realises that they recognise him but are trying to evade him, Strether's disenchantment begins. And his initiation into things French progresses rather sharply from this point. The first aspect of the liaison, as a liaison, which comes home to him is that it involves deception and betrayal of friends.

Even more significant for our purpose is the scene that

follows this encounter. Strether has returned to Paris with the lovers, who have tactfully maintained the pretence that they too were only out for the day, though there is glaring evidence to the contrary; but the next day Mme de Vionnet sends a message, asking him to call on her; and this last meeting between them is most revealing. At the moment when she comes in to greet him—and once again he feels the extraordinary charm of her presence—we read that

> . . . he knew in advance he should look back on the per-
> ception actually sharpest with him as on the view of
> something old, old, old, the oldest thing he had ever
> personally touched; and he also knew, even while he
> took his companion in as the feature among features,
> that memory and fancy couldn't help being enlisted
> for her. She might intend what she would, but this
> was beyond anything she could intend, with things
> from far back—tyrannies of history, facts of type, values,
> as the painters said, of expression—all working for her
> and giving her the supreme chance, the chance of the
> happy, the really luxurious few, the chance, on a great
> occasion, to be natural and simple.[3]

She expresses for him a whole tradition of manners and fine appearances: something at the heart of the Europe which is so fatal to Americans. But if he appreciates her as the most exquisite person he has ever known, she also appreciates the unworldly disinterestedness of his friend-ship, and is ashamed of her treatment of him: "Selfish and vulgar—that is what I must seem to you . . ." The scene culminates in the open confession of her plight, an involuntary tribute to him and his genuineness:

> He presently found himself taking a long look from her,
> and the next thing he knew he had uttered all his
> thought. "You're afraid for your life!"
>   It drew out her long look, and he soon enough saw

why. A spasm came into her face, the tears she had already been unable to hide overflowed at first in silence, and then, as the sound suddenly comes from a child, quickened to gasps, to sobs. She sat and covered her face with her hands, giving up all attempt at a manner . . . Her emotion was at first so incoherent that he could only stand there at a loss, stand with his sense of having upset her, though of having done it by the truth. He had to listen to her in a silence that he made no immediate effort to attenuate, feeling her doubly woeful amid all her dim diffused elegance; consenting to it as he had consented to the rest, and even conscious of some vague inward irony in the presence of such a fine free range of bliss and bale . . . She was older for him to-night, visibly less exempt from the touch of time; but she was as much as ever the finest and subtlest creature, the happiest apparition, it had been given him, in all his years, to meet; and yet he could see her there as vulgarly troubled, in very truth, as a maidservant crying for her young man.[4]

By letting the novel element of a New England consciousness into this old, old world of feelings and intrigues James throws fresh light on the familiar Parisian story, giving it unexpected poignancy.

If Strether represents sympathetic aspects of the New England outlook, he also represents characteristic defects. In one of the crucial passages in the book, the episode of Gloriani's party, he is overwhelmed by the sense of not having lived, and urges upon his young compatriot Little Bilham the lesson of seizing the day. Strether is, in fact, a slight case of Maule's curse. But his adventure in the novel itself is not really one of failing to live. Apart from his fine "vibrations" as an American in Europe, his capacity for romantic response, he shows his American flexibility in his acceptance of the new phenomenon presented by Chad; and, above all, when his illusions are destroyed, he adjusts himself to his fate with a modest dignity and resilience and a quaint irony which are also among the marks of his type.

The Wings of the Dove is James's tragic masterpiece, the richest and most moving of his works. It is a great sustained elegy for Minny Temple. In his Preface he refers to the theme as one which he had long cherished: "that of a young person conscious of a great capacity for life, but early stricken and doomed, condemned to die under short respite, while also enamoured of the world . . ." The question was how to treat it, and the answer he arrived at is a fine example of what is meant by definition of subject. The important point was that

> . . . the poet essentially *can't* be concerned with the act of dying. Let him deal with the sickest of the sick, it is still by the act of living that they appeal to him, and appeal the more as the conditions plot against them and prescribe the battle. The process of life gives way fighting, and often may so shine out on the lost ground as in no other connexion.[5]

James's presentation of Milly, in the light of this principle, has the greatest compositional beauty. Milly speaks as little as possible of her illness, and even when we see the action through her consciousness this factor is allowed only at necessary times to come to the surface. As in *What Maisie Knew* James's use of his heroine's consciousness is governed by a world of poetic proprieties. The same is true of his use of Mrs Stringham's consciousness in the first scenes which introduce Milly. For example, in the great episode where the anxious lady finds her young friend seated alone on the edge of an Alpine precipice, "looking down on the kingdoms of the world,"[6] and comes away without interrupting her, we do not know the reason for her original anxiety. The solemn prophetic passage which follows, expressing her intuition that what lies ahead for Milly is no "sharp or simple release from the human predicament," but "some more complicated passage," gives us our first unmistakable knowledge that Milly is a deeply troubled person. Mrs Stringham, of course, knows more than we do at this point, but her consciousness has been most discreetly and selectively used. (The artistic implications of this selectiveness are brilliantly analysed by Percy Lubbock, whose account of James's techniques is discussed in the final section of this essay.) References to doctors in the next chapter bring us nearer to the nature of the situation, but by this time an imaginative impression of Milly as a creature of rare and positive quality has been established. In one of the central passages of the book Milly visits the London specialist Sir Luke Strett and realises, not from any direct information he gives her but from his special note of benignity and consideration, that indeed her condition is bad. She keeps up the pretence, with him and later with others, that the main outcome of the visit is simply that she has gained another friend. After leaving him she wanders through the "grey immensity" of London ("Grey immensity had somehow of a sudden become her element"),[7] curiously buoyed up with her own courage, until she finds herself in Regent's Park; and there, on a common bench, conscious of others around her who are also facing the basic anxieties of life, and tired with her adventure, she can yet find a certain "charm" in the fact that no one knows where she is: it has never happened before, "so that she was now suddenly able to put it to herself that that hadn't been a life." It is impossible without much quoting to convey the exaltation and bravery, combined with what might be called the quaintness of Milly, in this supreme episode.

There are saving elements of contrast in the portrait. She has a touch of the American girl's verbal resourcefulness, in her early comments to Lord Mark. Mrs Stringham, a specialist in New Englandisms, occasionally notes some in Milly which serve to qualify the purely romantic aspect of her. It needs to be remembered that Mrs Stringham, who romanticises her the most and is responsible for the "princess" image of her, is a slightly comic figure and a bore to some of the other characters. In so far as we see Milly through the eyes of Densher, we see her—until his eyes have been opened—simply as the little American girl, not very exciting, but easy to get on with, as American girls are. (Matthiessen makes this point in his chapter on *The Wings of the Dove* in *Henry James: The Major Phase*.)

One of the consequences of James's method of presenting a situation in terms of the experience of one or more participants is that an objective retelling of the story, unless one is very careful, is liable to be a falsification and a frustration of the novelist's intention. The difference between events as they might look to an outsider who is given a summary of the "facts," and the same events from the point of view of a character who has lived through them, is crucial in James's novels. The relinquishing of moral prejudices on the part of the reader may be a necessary part of his response. Most synopses of *The Wings of the Dove* get the story wrong, either because the critic colours the facts with his own moral idiom or simply because in his ordering of them he misses the atmosphere and emphasis which are essential to James's treatment. But how difficult it is to retell the last part of this novel without destroying what the novelist has built up!

These last sections are Densher's experience, and we must feel his bewilderment and pain before we try to make diagrams of motives, actions, and consequences. The central figure in Densher's experience is, of course, Kate; and no skill in retelling can do justice to the effect of her presence. It is sometimes assumed that, with their greater freedom, twentieth-century novelists can show more of the nature of sexual love than their unfortunate predecessors could; but the power of the bond between lovers

has not often been so movingly conveyed as it is here.
When Densher becomes aware of Kate's intentions, his
awareness of her as the person with whom he is agonis-
ingly in love remains dominant; and nothing that happens, nothing that follows from Kate's intentions, renders
her less appealing to him or to us. Densher becomes pain-
fully conscious that there are things Kate cannot appreciate: she has a capacity for ignoring certain aspects of a
human situation. It is with compassion for both of them
that we see what has come between them by the end of
the story.

Kate's scheme, isolated from our sense of her as a person, goes rather unpleasantly into words. But if in the
synopsis it looks sordid, in the novel itself there is a kind
of desperate heroism about it. A defence of Kate would
take into account the fact that earlier in her career she
proved her superiority to mere sordidness by giving away
half of her small income to her sister; but such arguments
on her behalf are not quite to the point. What is re-
quired (and what the novel gives), is that we should see
her as Densher sees her, and see him as under her spell.
The fact that Kate is willing, as it were, to *lend* him to
Milly, to allow him to become Milly's husband for the
short time that is left to her, strikes Densher mainly as
disturbing evidence of her strength of purpose and forti-
tude. For him it is a terrible violence to their love, and he
cannot finally agree to it unless Kate does one thing for
him: she must first come to his rooms and allow him to
possess her. This is no easy thing for her, but she does it.
Densher's preoccupation with Kate, together with the
fact that Milly from the outset has been fond of him, so
that the issue of not disappointing her must arise in one
form or another, together with subsidiary facts, such as
the encouragement of Sir Luke Strett and Mrs Stringham,
who want Milly to be happy, and that of Mrs Lowder,
who has other plans for Kate: all this has the effect of
preventing the cruder fortune-hunting aspects of his be-

haviour from occupying the foreground of his mind as revealed to us. Fortune-hunting is what he becomes committed to, yet he is never presented to us as having settled down to the idea of it; and the more specific perjuries have still not been uttered when Lord Mark's disclosure to Milly puts an end to everything.

The effect of Milly's last meeting with him—we are given only Densher's retrospective glimpse of it—is that she sends him away with thoughts of her which destroy the completeness of his allegiance to Kate. Some critics take the view that Densher has undergone a religious experience of the order of Christian redemption. His own recollection of it is expressed in the words: "He had been, to his recovered sense, forgiven, dedicated, blessed . . ."[9] What can really be said is that Milly has given him thoughts of ineffable and haunting tenderness, when he might have had degrading ones. He cannot avoid pain on account of Milly, but he is represented as suffering higher pains than those of remorse. And part of the pain is that what Milly has given him cannot, by its very nature, be shared with Kate. There is a passage in the last chapter in which his thoughts of Milly, relating to her last letter which an anguished scruple has forbidden him to read, are described: a passage to marvel at, with its strange wild images and overwhelming pathos. This is what she has done for him, but what can he do with it, except cherish it as long as it will last? Densher's desire is that it shall last as long as it can, though he knows that time is the destroyer of even the rarest thoughts. He has been changed from a straight-forward lover into a man of reveries. Kate tells him that Milly's memory is now his love, and that he needs no other.

The imaginative and moral design of this novel seems to require that Kate and Densher should be presented to us in terms of all that is positive in their situation, which means that certain aspects, those that figure prominently in many critical summaries, do not appear. The point-of-view technique is the instrument of generosity. It is something that in the defeat of their happiness at the end they should have so much beauty in their lives. The last and most eloquent tribute to Milly is spoken by Kate herself in a scene of monumental quality.

The Golden Bowl, though immensely brilliant in parts, is more difficult to accept as a whole than the other two great novels of this period. It is a question of the balance of our sympathies. We know from the Notebook sketch that it was James's intention that the father and daughter should be regarded as the wronged and innocent parties, and that the liaison between their respective marriage partners should be viewed as treachery; but many readers are unsatisfied with the Ververs and sympathise with the Prince and Charlotte. It is the second half of the book, where we follow Maggie's victory through her own vision of it, that raises the chief difficulties. Some readers see the Ververs as symbols of goodness, others as examples of the emotional and moral inadequacy of the American plutocrat. The first part is easier to come to terms with, though it is not always as much enjoyed as it might be.

As we read the first pages of *The Golden Bowl* we begin to explore imaginatively a situation as it takes shape in the mind of Amerigo, the young Italian Prince. It is a situation to stimulate the imagination: the girl he is going to marry is the daughter of a fabulously rich American. All readers notice the frequency and lavishness of the images relating to wealth and costly *objets d'art* in these pages, and some are repelled by this atmosphere of opulence. But the tone of the opening depends on the almost humorous charm of the situation as it appears to the Prince—and to the novelist, for whom the charm is more complex. Maggie and her father are so very unsophisticated; they are almost impossibly cheerful and friendly and vague, the embodiment of the famous American "good faith." The prospect they offer the Prince of limitless material abundance, with nothing to do except to be himself—as an Italian Prince he is a unique object—is a dream to which he submits with just that element of amused appreciation that prevents the idea from being cloying to us. James multiplies and inflates and embellishes his images of wealth with a kind of wanton virtuosity. There is an element of effrontery in it. There is provocation in the fact that Maggie should be so rich and should enjoy it so openly. It is appalling, or so it might seem, that she should refer to her *fiancé* as a museum piece, one of the rarities that "can only be got over here"—that is, in Europe. But Maggie can say these things, with her absurd frankness and freshness: James gets away with it. Essentially this is a situation in which everyone is as nice as possible to everyone else. The novelty of the American outlook to the Italian, and *vice versa*, give rise only to comfortable little understandings and quaint expressions of mutual accommodation.

The novel has been the occasion for so much moral, sociological, thematic, and symbolical analysis that readers may miss the simple and delightful fact that in the early stages it is largely comedy: social comedy of a very high order in some places, using as its material the steepest of contrasts and the most extreme incongruities. The Ververs, with all their wealth, are in several respects typically helpless Americans. Three episodes may be singled out to illustrate this. In the first, Mr Verver is caught trying to escape from one of his female guests at his country house. Being a friendly, obliging person, much too easy of access, he finds it difficult to protect himself from encroachment, so he takes refuge in the billiard-room; but the relentless Mrs Rance follows him there, and it is at this significant moment that Maggie and the others arrive home from church to witness his embarrassment. It is not unimportant that the moment of suspense for Mr Verver, as he enters the billiard-room, is chosen by the novelist as the occasion for a long backward glance over his career, with discursive reflexions on his charac-

ter and aspirations: a passage full of wit, and also of a
kind of penetration which some critics have found destruc-
tive. There are indeed references to his past life as a
brilliantly successful business-man, to "the creation of
'interests' that were the extinction of other interests, the
livid vulgarity, even, of getting in, or getting out, first."[10]
And there are many hints and suggestions that such a life
as this has involved emotional and spiritual impoverish-
ments, but we need to savour the prose in which they are
conveyed. Read as a whole, and as a digression from the
place of all places in the plot where Mr Verver is presented as a mild, gentle figure, discomfited because he
just cannot be unkind, the effect of these strokes will be
modified. If there are contradictions here, James would
seem to have planted them deliberately. If we do not like
the idea that Mr Verver is nice, perhaps we must lump it.

After the billiard-room scene there is a long conversation between Maggie and her father, in which the important question of his marrying again is brought up; and
this, though an affectionate scene, has an element of
comedy in it. Maggie says that, at least according to their
friends, their social life is a little on the meagre side. Mr
Verver has never noticed this, and Maggie herself is only
just discovering it. Simple, undemanding creatures as
they are, they are slow to realise that the Assinghams, and
Dotty and Kitty Lutch, to say nothing of Mrs Rance, are
a somewhat unimpressive collection of associates for
people with their range of opportunity. "The thing is,"
she says, ". . . that I don't think we lead, as regards other
people, any life at all."[11] Mr Verver wonders what sort of
life people expect them to lead; to which Maggie's reply
is that Fanny Assingham thinks they ought to be
"greater." But her father's only response to this is to
echo the word in a questioning manner. And then, later,
she asserts that, "If we ought to be grander, as Fanny
thinks, we *can* be grander. There's nothing to prevent."
The vagueness of the expressions, the references to Fanny,

as if she were the touchstone of social sophistication, give the measure of Maggie's slender awareness of what is missing; and they make an engagingly quaint couple as they sit there, trying very patiently to understand their problem. The immense gulf between so much wealth and so little capacity for what, in a worldly sense, may be referred to as "life," is one of the comic themes of this part of the novel. Maggie and her father reach a conclusion; namely, that Charlotte Stant can help them. A capacity for life is precisely what she has. So Charlotte is, to use their easy turn of phrase, "called in."

The last episode of the three is as spectacular in aspect as the others are homely. The setting is the grand staircase of a splendid house, the occasion a reception, the central figure Charlotte (now Mrs Verver), looking her wonderful best. The Prince is there too, and both of them are showing their capacity for life. But where are the Ververs? At home, looking after the little boy! The comedy takes on a florid complexion as Charlotte's public appearance with the Prince comes to the notice of Fanny Assingham—who, as the architect of the Prince's marriage, has it on her conscience that she has always known what Maggie doesn't know; namely, that the Prince and Charlotte had been in love at an earlier stage. Fanny has a spirited exchange with Charlotte, who is formidable; and then there is a different kind of exchange with the Prince, who, with all the charm and good-nature in the world, explains that, after all, life at home does make one sometimes pant for a little change of air. Fanny likes the Prince, but she "continues to fly the black flag of general repudiation."[12] Critics have varied in their views of Fanny. It seems a pity to take her too seriously. She and her husband, the delicious Colonel, are in fact splendid comic creations. As Fanny listens to the Prince's charmingly persuasive talk, we read that

there was not a drop of it that she didn't, in a manner,

catch, as it came, for immediate bottling, for future preservation. The crystal flask of her innermost attention really received it on the spot, and she had even already the vision of how, in the snug laboratory of her afterthought, she should be able chemically to analyse it.[13]

The turn of expression sufficiently indicates James's attitude to her habits of thought and speech. It is in her late evening communings with the Colonel that Fanny indulges her analytical vein. The Colonel is laconic and unimaginative: "his short cuts, always across her finest flower-beds,"[14] provoke her impatience.

The first part of the novel is rich in these elements of the portentous and the comic. The second part, with its remarkable succession of dramatic scenes, also portentous but at another level, contains problems calling for lengthier treatment than is possible here. Some reference to them will be made in the concluding chapter where James's critics are discussed.

It has been suggested that some features of James's later style are due to his habit of dictation, which began as a result of a disabled hand in the late eighteen-nineties. Whatever the significance of this factor, the later prose is more colloquial than the earlier and also more elaborate. The elaborateness should not be regarded as an expression of any such quality of mind in the character whose consciousness is being explored. James's centres of consciousness are often rather naïve, bewildered people; but this in itself is not the point. The ramifying prose expresses his sense of the organic growth of an imaginative response, or of its exploratory character. Through this style the novelist himself is present as interpreter, sometimes near to his character, seeing the situation virtually in the latter's terms, and at other times further removed, allowing his poetic imagination, his humour, or his rhetoric scope to shape the situation more freely, but always with consideration for the character's central position and point of view. At all times it is the style of a writer who cherishes his subject personally, and this feeling communicates itself to the reader.

In *The American Scene* (1907) a rather heightened form of this style is used to express the assault of America upon James's mind and sensibility after a more than twenty years' absence. James treats his own experience in a similar way to that of his fictitious characters. As far as possible it is the full impact that he seeks to convey, the intellect at work from the outset upon the visual spectacle but not in such a way as to spoil its freshness or lessen its appeal to a sense of wonder. It is a book of astonishing power and eloquence, far beyond the earlier travel books in the brilliance of the impressions and in the seriousness of his concern with the human aspects of the places he is visiting. He responds with delight and affection to what is still recognisable of the old America, but is baffled and disturbed by evidences in the new America of great wealth divorced from any sense of how to live.

Had he been a younger man, the effect of this visit on his treatment of American themes in fiction would no doubt have been very substantial. Such as it was it manifested itself promptly in "The Jolly Corner" (1908), a horror story in which the central character, a returned expatriate, is obsessed by the thought of what he would have become had he stayed in America and plunged into its business life. After much lying in wait he finally encounters this *alter ego*, who turns out to be a totally alien and dreadful figure. "A Round of Visits" (1910), his last story, also deals with the return of an expatriate to an America riddled with business corruption. The hero of the unfinished novel, *The Ivory Tower* (1917), is another sensitive, cultivated exile, brought back to inherit a millionaire's fortune in a Newport now disfigured by the monstrous houses of the newly rich. One of the unforgettable images of its early chapters is that of the rival millionaire, terrible little Abel Gaw, with his utterly dehumanised old age and fixed predatory expression. James's other unfinished novel, *The Sense of the Past* (1917), is in neat contrast, having as hero the most deeply committed of passionate pilgrims in Europe. Ralph Pendrel's preparedness for Europe is more specialised than that of his predecessors: he is an historian, and he carries his obsession with England to the point not only of an insatiable drinking-in of impressions but of a stepping-back into its history.

Between 1907 and 1909 the twenty-four volumes of the New York edition of his novels and tales appeared. James had hopes that this venture would bring him prosperity, but he was disappointed. Opinions differ considerably on the value of his very extensive revisions for this edition. The famous Prefaces, written specially for it, are liable to be misunderstood, both by readers who respect him as a supreme exponent of method in the novel and by those who rebel against method. He often admitted, it is true, that he could not read other people's novels without wanting to re-write them; but he said this apologetically, and believed at heart that people should write in their own way, and that one of the great virtues of the novel as a form was that it gave scope for variety and individuality. Some of the best-known passages in the Prefaces, on such topics as economy of form and the relation between art and life, are liable to be given the wrong emphasis unless they are read in their context of happy reflexion on actual solutions to his own problems. The Prefaces are in fact essentially autobiographical. He is concerned rather with telling how the subject for a novel came his way, and how it took shape in his imagination, than with doctrinaire theorising. It is true that, in a letter to Howells, he did refer to them collectively as a kind of treatise for the guidance of practitioners, but only one side of James is represented by such a remark. We appreciate them best if we respond to their elements of humour and extravagance.

Any discussion of James's theoretical views on the novel should be related to his criticism of other novelists. As a critic he is at his best when he kindles to writers of huge scope and massive subject-matter, such as Balzac and Zola. Some of his tastes would not please the more austere of his modern admirers. He had an unquenchable interest in George Sand, on whom he produced several essays, and he wrote very favourably on Trollope in the essay referred to earlier. His impatience with the looseness of the traditional English novel is, again, only one aspect of him. His tributes to the power of Dickens in *A Small Boy and Others* and *Notes of a Son and a Brother* need to be read in this connexion.

Of the autobiographies, the main achievement of his latest years, and an expression surely of deep fulfilment, no more needs to be said here.

The Henry James of the final period is not a personality to be dismissed with a brief description. It is necessary to read the testimony of many friends and acquaintances, and fortunately we have a delightful collection in Simon Nowell-Smith's *The Legend of the Master*. His kindness, his humour, his voluminous eloquence: these are among the aspects which most frequently recur in the many stories that survive. His friends included Edith Wharton, A. C. Benson, Edmund Gosse, Mrs Humphrey Ward, and later, Hugh Walpole. To Conrad he was *cher maître*, to Ford Madox Hueffer (Ford) the greatest man in the world. Of his letters of this period none are more instructive than the series of cordial outpourings of praise to H. G. Wells, a writer so different from himself in every respect. Wells's satirical treatment of him in *Boon* (1915), apart from being an atrociously ungenerous act, is perhaps the most conspicuous expression of an all too common failure at this period to appreciate what James was trying to do.

The outbreak of war in 1914 was a tremendous shock to him, but he responded to it positively. He came to live in London, visited wounded soldiers and gave help to

Belgian refugees. A series of essays written on behalf of various wartime causes were collected in the little posthumous volume *Within the Rim* (1919). In 1915 he demonstrated his attitude by becoming naturalised as a British subject. He died in the following year.

REFERENCES

1. *Amb.*, p. 322.
2. *Amb.*, p. 327.
3. *Amb.*, p. 339.
4. *Amb.*, pp. 344–5.
5. *W.D.*, I, p. vii.
6. *W.D.*, I, p. 111.
7. *W.D.*, I, p. 218.

8. *W.D.*, I, p. 221.
9. *W.D.*, II, p. 305.
10. *G.B.*, p. 101.
11. *G.B.*, p. 123.
12. *G.B.*, p. 189.
13. *G.B.*, p. 190.
14. *G.B.*, p. 261.

CHAPTER VII

JAMES AND HIS CRITICS

To do justice to Henry James, to convey any adequate impression of the quality and quantity of pleasure his work can give, one would need a prose as rich and vehement as his own; and indeed in such places as the Preface to *What Maisie Knew*, he wrote much better about himself than any of his critics have done. Apart from the inadequacy of summaries and the impoverishment suffered by passages divorced from their context, the critic of James has the special problem of how to represent abundance without becoming tedious. The abundance of James's writings, together with their extraordinarily high standard, is a literary phenomenon to which it would be difficult to find a parallel in modern times.

A sense of proportion is one of the first requirements of both the critic and the literary biographer, but there are many factors in the task itself which militate against the exercise of this virtue. The greatness of an artist's work sets the standard to which everything else in one's account of him ought to be adjusted; but faults or difficulties, through their very complexity or their theoretical interest, demand and tend to receive a disproportionate treatment. The biographer, as custodian of the facts, has the double responsibility of giving full weight to the evidence and, at the same time, of ensuring that the total effect is worthy of his subject. Certain aspects of James's life—his remaining a bachelor, for example, and his decision to live in Europe—are very liable to give rise to discussion which distorts the reader's attitude to his works. The difficulty of some of the novels provokes many readers not to try again but rather to put the blame on James's personal development, while those readers who are satisfied with the works in question may be content with a different biographical theory. Literary biography is an extremely mixed and hazardous art. Attitudes to a writer's books continually colour the facts of his life and *vice versa*. One of the biographer's problems is that the books exist somehow in a different perspective from the other facts. And the relation between a writer's artistic successes or failures and the quality of the rest of his life is obscure.

Van Wyck Brooks's *The Pilgrimage of Henry James* (1925) is the study of a deluded expatriate, who never really grasped his Europe and ended by having no country of his own. It contains favourable estimates of the novels of the middle period, but dismisses James's later manner with impatience. This seems to be an example of the typical confusion that literary biography can lead to. Brooks may have been limited by not having available the wealth of anecdotes and other materials that have since become current: certainly his selection gives a one-sided impression; but what does most to give the story its hollow, negative effect is his own failure to make anything important of James's late works. The comment on the books then becomes a comment on the life, though a prejudice about expatriates may have prepared the way for a dislike of the books.

Modern students looking for a short life of James are more likely to come across F. W. Dupee's *Henry James* (1951) and this is very much better. A book which tries to deal critically with both life and works in a moderately sized volume is bound to be sketchy in places, but within its limits this is a remarkably successful attempt. Dupee writes handsomely about the later phase of James's life. Leon Edel's *Henry James: The Untried Years* (1953) is the first instalment of a biography which will revolutionise our knowledge of the subject, by a scholar to whom all students of James owe a multitude of debts. But it illustrates in several places not only the problems inherent in literary biography but also certain procedures which may be regarded as questionable. Early in *A Small Boy and Others* James refers to the effect on him of William's seniority by sixteen months, and Edel draws upon this passage as evidence of frustration in Henry's childhood; but somehow in its context the passage does not convey this impression so strongly as one might gather from Edel's use of it. In the autobiographies James was not much concerned with frustrations. Whatever the experiences may have meant at the time—and this, of course, is the biographer's concern—they are absorbed into a narrative dominated by the happy feeling that his was a wonderfully privileged childhood. Here we have a question concerning the relation between biography and autobiography. It is the biographer's task to supplement the autobiographical record, and sometimes to suggest changes of emphasis, but this calls for considerable care. If James's narrative minimised the tensions between William and himself—this is possible—Edel's method is to give them greater prominence by speculating on their influence on the themes of the novels and stories. He writes:

> Readers of Henry James's novels and tales discover at every turn the writer's predilection for second sons. Sometimes he kills off elder brothers or turns them into villains; sometimes his hero is an only son, usually with a widowed mother. He thus confers on them an ideal fatherless and brotherless state.[1]

Psychological connexions between an author's work and his life are likely to be complex and need tactful handling. Such comments as the above have the effect of heightening the narrative, but the contribution they make to our knowledge remains unclear. In discussing the later relations of the two brothers, Edel develops the uncanny theory that Henry's health in his twenties improved when William was away and deteriorated on the latter's return, and certainly the evidence cannot be ignored; but again he exploits his point excessively.

Our attitude to James's life must depend partly on objective facts ascertainable by scholarship, but literary judgment is also involved in so far as we may respond in different ways to the tone of the autobiographies and letters. Both in *The Untried Years* and in his remarks elsewhere on the letters, Edel seems to be rather cautious in his response to a generosity and benignity in James's writing to which other readers would kindle.

It is difficult to see any clear pattern in the history of critical opinion on James. In some respects, Joseph Warren Beach's book *The Method of Henry James* (1918) has never been surpassed as an inclusive treatment of technique, while Percy Lubbock's passages on James in *The Craft of Fiction* (1921) contain easily the most brilliant attempt ever made to describe a particular aspect of his technique: the use of the point of view. Yet critical opinion in general was slow to realise James's magnitude, and he has only gradually come into his own.

Beach's book has its limitations from the viewpoint of the modern reader. It appeared before criticism was put on its mettle by the moral and methodological challenges of recent times, and is very much an impersonal academic performance. It will be of most use to those readers of James whose minds are already engaged by the great questions his work raises. Beach deals very thoroughly, if rather coolly, with many aspects of James's technique, and is one of the few critics who have analysed the function of his dialogue.

Lubbock gives not only an excellent analysis of technique, but also an eloquent tribute to its success. He chooses *The Ambassadors* as his chief example. After showing why it is so appropriate that Strether's story should be presented from his own point of view, he makes the subtle observation that though this point of view gives us, as it were, the "material" of his experience—we see what he sees—it no longer operates when we are shown what he does with his experience. According to Lubbock, Strether's mind is "dramatised" for us. Its contents—impulses and reactions and so forth—are exhibited as if they were actors on a stage. We are given only the "outer aspect of his mind"—if we can imagine a mind made visible; we do not penetrate below the surface, so that it is not all given away to us: "there is no need for it to yield up all its secrets at once."[2] There is, in fact, as much opportunity for delays and suspense as in any other drama:

> To bring his mind into view at the different moments, one after another, when it is brushed by new experience—to make a little scene of it, without breaking into hidden depths where the change of purpose is proceeding—to multiply these glimpses until the silent change is apparent, though no word has actually been said of it: this is Henry James's way . . .[3]

It is "devious and roundabout," yet finally it produces the most direct effect, "for the reader has seen."

To describe how an artist achieves his purpose, in language in some degree worthy of the achievement, is a difficult and unusual feat, and Lubbock's account of James stands by itself. Where it may call for qualification perhaps is in his comparison of the novelist to a playwright, who leaves his characters to act out their parts without his intervention. This hardly makes allowance for James's prose style, with its characteristically personal interpretative tone. A possible solution would be to say that James's tone is that of a *spectator* of this drama: that it is he who appreciates it and shares it with us, so that, far from disappearing, the novelist is as pervasively present as in any other kind of fiction. This point, if acceptable, need not conflict with Lubbock's analysis. It adds one more advantage to those that he claims.

It is unfortunate that in two of the best-known general studies of the novel by distinguished men of letters in the years following Lubbock's book, James does not receive very serious or sympathetic treatment. E. M. Forster, in *Aspects of the Novel* (1927), writes agreeably on *The Ambassadors* but refers with approval to H. G. Wells's miserable travesty of James in *Boon*, and accepts the crude and misleading opposition of Art and Life which the Wellsian position encourages. This is a large and complex subject. James responded to the life in Wells's novels as fully as anyone has done, one of his main objections to his technique being that, by the use of an autobiographical hero, Wells deprived other characters of some of the reality and life that they ought to have had. As for the life in James's novels, there are, briefly, two lines of defence: the first, which stresses the qualitative factor, the intensity and fineness of the "felt life" in his best work; and the second, which calls attention to the breadth of social reference in his work as a whole, which is surely not contemptible even by the standards of a Wells! Edwin Muir, in *The Structure of the Novel* (1928), follows Forster in regretting the exclusion of so much life from a James novel, and associates him with mere neatness of arrangement. He also accuses Lubbock of narrowness in his attitude to form and in his preference for James. Elementary justice demands that Lubbock should be recognised as an enthusiastic interpreter not only of James but also of writers as different from him as Thackerary and Dickens. Both James and Lubbock are generous and inclusive in their tastes in the novel. Lubbock never said that all novelists should write like James, but recognised the appropriateness of different methods for different novels.

James's American critics have always been especially interested in him, for better or for worse, as an interpreter of American life, and both T. S. Eliot and Ezra Pound, in their essays of 1918 and 1920 respectively, testified to his excellence in this respect. Constance Rourke's chapter on James, in her distinguished study *American Humour* (1931), is refreshing after the solemnity of so many of his critics. She helps to counteract the common emphasis on expatriate limitations by stressing James's early acquaintance with the popular American tradition; and with this in mind she comments well, as was noted earlier, on *The American*. One of her most acute observations relates to characters not usually associated with comedy, to whom she attributes what she terms a "low-keyed humour of defeat." Strether is not mentioned in this context, but the phrase fits him very well. Yvor Winters's essay on James, which appears as a chapter in *Maule's Curse* (1938), is mainly an exploration of the role in his work of a moral sense derived from the New England tradition but rarefied to the point almost of dissolution and divorced from definite doctrine. He discusses a number of moral situations in the novels, and finds them obscure and unsatisfying. Yet he concludes by saying that he is the greatest novelist in English. In spite of some imperfections in the treatment of ethical issues James triumphs, in his opinion, through his unequalled wealth of characters. This is an unusual tribute and worth noting.

There have been several attempts to relate the moral content of James's novels to the ideas of Emerson and his generation. In Philip Rahv's valuable essay "The Heiress of all the Ages," the conflict between Isabel and Osmond is placed in this context. Isabel he sees as the Emersonian Young American, and it is this aspect of her that is peculiarly offensive to Osmond, who has developed a false, non-American traditionalism and despises what he calls the note of the "radical newspaper" or the "Unitarian preacher." But the most elaborate analysis of this kind is Quentin Anderson's *The American Henry*

James (1958). Anderson's thesis is that James's novels are the artistic exemplification of the ideas of his father. His theory is much respected by some of James's best critics, and whether one accepts it or not it certainly bears the stamp of a first-rate mind. I am obliged to confess myself totally unable to accept it. However much it may appear to be supported by the text, it seems to me untrue to the tone of James's writings. But this is a book which should either be discussed at very great length or not at all.

Another aspect of his Americanness is his relation to Hawthorne. This was touched upon in T. S. Eliot's essay, and was further developed in F. O. Matthiessen's *American Renaissance* (1941), and again, very usefully, in Marius Bewley's *The Complex Fate* (1952). It is interesting to see what happens when critics try to place James significantly in the pattern of development of the American novel. Richard Chase's main thesis in *The American Novel and its Tradition* (1957) is that the American novel differs from the English in its more extensive use of romance; or, going deeper, that whereas the English novel is concerned with a stable English social order, the American novel exploits the contradictions and disharmonies of the culture which produced it. He stresses the elements of romance and melodrama in James (Jaques Barzun's useful article "Henry James: Melodramatist" may be read in this connexion), though he recognises also that, in places like the opening chapters of *The Portrait of a Lady*, we have a realisation of the other side of the novelist's art: observation of man in the framework of a social order. He agrees with F. R. Leavis in seeing him as a "poet-novelist." James for him combines the strengths of both the American and the English traditions. Chase's attitude to James is very reasonable but, of course, the scheme of his book does not give him much opportunity to show to what tune James was a master of the novel of manners, a form which he treats as very far from central to the American tradition. His interesting chapter on *The

Portrait of a Lady stresses the poetic aspects, notably the imagery. It is absolutely right, of course, that James should be placed in this tradition, but it is difficult to do it without either digressing from the main stream of the tradition or giving a diminished impression of his greatness. For example, what is such an historian to do with *The Tragic Muse* or *What Maisie Knew*?

No contribution has been more influential than Edmund Wilson's "The Ambiguity of Henry James" (1934), which is chiefly known for its elaboration of the theory that the governess in "The Turn of the Screw" is hallucinated. An essay by Harold C. Goddard, published posthumously in 1957, is perhaps the earliest statement of this view, and there has been much debate on the subject; but this is not the most important kind of ambiguity discussed by Wilson. In several of James's novels and stories a type recurs which may be referred to as the "inquisitive observer"—the narrator in *The Sacred Fount* is the most egregious specimen—and Wilson argues that in some cases James is not sufficiently aware of his obnoxious aspects, being confessedly an inquisitive observer himself. Another dubious moral type is the refined, well-to-do American who avoids the vulgarity of the world where money is made. Wilson's theory, which is akin to that of Van Wyck Brooks, is that absence from America and incomplete understanding of Europe had an unfortunate effect on James's sense of values, leading to an "inability sometimes to be clear as to what he wants us to think about a certain sort of person."[4] This links up with Winters's objections to some of the moral situations in James. Wilson here opens up an important field of enquiry. The main defect of his essay, however, is a rather hostile tone, which shows itself in such passages as that in which he includes Milly among the women who long for affection but are "too inhibited or passive to obtain it for themselves."[5] Bewley's contribution on ambiguity is very interesting. For him an uncertainty "as to what is appearance and what is reality, or how to distinguish between truth and falsehood, or how to bring evil to a particular focus"[6] is an American characteristic. He has a neat answer for critics like Wilson who say that, owing to his residence abroad, James became "incapable of distinguishing between a gentleman and cad":

> Cads and gentlemen are made such by the social perspective in which they exist, and in viewing any given context of appearance and reality James developed an astigmatism that was essentially American. The fault that the critics deplore is not due to the fact that James stayed abroad too long, but that he didn't get out of America soon enough.[7]

But Bewley shows that James could sometimes control the ambiguous element in situations: his analyses of the two stories "The Path of Duty" and "The Liar" bring this out very well. In some cases it may be felt that the moral value of the reader's experience lies in the fact that the behaviour of the characters has not been so portrayed as to invite the moralist to apply his labels. This seems to be true of James's treatment of Kate and Densher.

Matthiessen's *Henry James: The Major Phase* (1944) is less concerned with special approaches and problems than with the central task of presenting James as a great and dedicated artist, and vindicating the later phase in answer to such writers as Van Wyck Brooks. It is a generous and civilised book, and one of the two or three indispensable critical studies. He writes well on the three culminating novels and he is our best guide to James's subsequent work: *The American Scene*, the unfinished novels, and the late stories. His volume includes an essay on the revisions of *The Portrait of a Lady*, with an important discussion of the implications of its ending. As co-editor, with Kenneth B. Murdock, of James's Notebooks, which appeared some years later, Matthiessen was able to show a deep personal knowledge of his artistic attitudes and habits.

The most important general estimate of James by an English critic is, of course, that of F.R. Leavis in *The Great Tradition* (1948) and elsewhere. Leavis shows a preference for, and writes admirably about, works like *The Europeans*, *Washington Square* and, more especially, *The Portrait of a Lady* and *The Bostonians*, which belong to what he calls the "sappiest phase" of his art, though he gives high praise also to some of the later novels, such as *What Maisie Knew* and *The Awkward Age*. He admires most the James who shows the virtues of the tradition he is tracing, but is less sympathetic to the side of him which responds to certain romantic elements in the contemporary American ethos. This may involve some unfairness to James in his dealings with relatively new national ideas and types. In comparing the "idealised" Isabel Archer with the more solid Gwendolen Harleth of *Daniel Deronda* he does not sufficiently acknowledge the pioneering originality of the former portrait. He exaggerates the romanticism in James's attitude when he complains that he is uncritical of Isabel and her idealism:

> We can't even say that James makes an implicit critical comment on the background of American idealism that fostered her romantic confidence in life and in her ability to choose: he admires her so much and demands for her such admiration and homage, that he can't be credited with 'placing' the conditions that, as an admirable American girl, she represents.[8]

This calls for detailed discussion of the passages, cited earlier, where Isabel's faults are stated, and also of those episodes—for example, the crucial conversation with Ralph about Osmond—where her confidence and independence are shown as an inadequate equipment for the decisions which confront her. Leavis's standards in these matters are high, but he is not wholly just here.

Leavis is, in general, unfavourable to the late novels, notably *The Ambassadors*, which he simply dismisses as bad. His view is akin to that of Van Wyck Brooks: James's development went wrong, and his grasp of reality was affected. But one of his comments on *The Ambassadors* seems to point to a limitation in himself:

What, we ask, is this, symbolized by Paris, that Strether feels himself to have missed in his own life? Has James himself sufficiently inquired?[9]

Behind such questions is a lack of feeling for passionate pilgrims and beguiled Americans generally. Whatever the moral implications of Strether's experience, the spell of Paris is surely conveyed to perfection. If one looked for elements of genuine worth in Strether's Paris, compared with his Woollett, it would not be impossible to find them, but what is more relevant is the effect on him of certain appearances which speak to him of freer and fuller living. If this is vague, it is in keeping with the nature of the American romantic response. But Strether is not vague all the time, and before the end of the book his Gloriani mood has fallen into its place and he has learnt much.

Admirers of the later books will not be wholly satisfied with Leavis's work, but with all its limitations it has been of decisive value in placing James among the very great novelists in English.

Brief reference may be made here to a few criticisms of individual novels and special aspects. Of all his works, except "The Turn of the Screw," the most controversial is *The Golden Bowl*. Ferner Nuhn imagines how the story would look from Charlotte's viewpoint. Leavis prefers the "decent passion"[10] of Charlotte and the Prince to the life of the Ververs, in what he describes as the "stale, sickly and oppressive atmosphere" of the book. Matthiessen complains that there is a lack of moral truth in the portrait of Adam Verver, traceable to James's ignorance of the turpitude of the contemporary business world; and he calls attention also to the dubiousness of the father-daughter relationship. Philip Rahv, in "Attitudes to Henry James," agrees to some extent with these views, but makes a good comment on the imaginative vitality with which the opulent Verver world is realised. J. J. Firebaugh, in his essay "The Ververs," goes further than other critics in his condemnation of the inhumanity of both father and daughter. Apart from making too much of Maggie's tyrannical possessiveness (Charlotte is possessive too—it is that kind of situation!) Firebaugh fails to give the most striking evidence of Maggie's compassion for Charlotte: the remarkable "golden flame" passage.[11] The value of Firebaugh's essay is that it counteracts the excessively exalted view of this pair held not only by Quentin Anderson but by such critics as R. P. Blackmur. The fact that it has given occasion for such violent differences of opinion seems to suggest something unresolved in the novel itself. Perhaps there is a lack of appeal in Maggie during her phase of struggle. And it seems unfortunate, at the level of plotting, that victory should be so manifestly with those who have power to arrange everything as they wish. On the other hand, it may be argued that this was just the kind of technical obstacle that James enjoyed overcoming, and that we are intended to accept the Ververs in spite of everything. In the remarkable last chapter, where Charlotte and the Prince are "placed" among all the furniture and "pieces," virtually "human furniture" themselves, James almost invites us to see them as "concrete attestations of a rare power of purchase,"[12] a view which would support Firebaugh's analysis: but in referring to this view as "more penetrating than the occasion really demanded," he is perhaps withholding the invitation, and leaving the moral advantage with the Ververs after all. It is a witty passage, but not easy to interpret with certainty.

The Portrait of a Lady has been fortunate in its critics. There is an excellent essay by Arnold Kettle, and Ernest

Sandeen's comparative study of this novel with *The Wings of the Dove* is one of the best pieces of Jamesian criticism of recent years. L. C. Knights and Allen Tate have written admirably on "The Beast in the Jungle." Important discussions of *The Sacred Fount* have been produced by Leon Edel and Miriam Allott. Lionel Trilling's most attractive essay on *The Princess Casamassima* demonstrates the accuracy of James's treatment of the revolutionary theme, and in his interpretation of Hyacinth's role he attributes to the novel a quality of tragedy which some readers may feel is lacking. Trilling has written also on *The Bostonians*. In both books he sees rather more of the social critic in James than may be warranted, but a little exaggeration in this direction is understandable in view of the lack of attention hitherto paid to this aspect of him. *What Maisie Knew*, which was rather neglected or underrated by earlier critics, has recently come into its own. Bewley ranks it as the greatest of the late novels; Leavis has written well on it, in response to Bewley's rather wayward interpretation; and there is a very rewarding account of it by William Walsh. Blackmur's scholarly introduction to the Prefaces (*The Art of the Novel*) is indispensable, though he misses something of their spirit in his rigorous concern with points of abstract principle. Leon Edel's introduction to his edition of the plays is a thorough study of James's dealings with the theatre.

A good deal of criticism on James takes the form of abstract speculation on the nature of his art and its relevance to modern culture. One of the most suggestive essays of this kind is Blackmur's "The Loose and Baggy Monsters of Henry James" (1951), which concludes with reflexions on the "burden of consciousness" placed upon the individual as the result of the decay of culture as a social fact. Blackmur sees this phenomenon as the relevant background for James's novels, especially those in which the consciousness of the central characters is most highly cultivated. This essay is of exceptional value, but on the whole the tendency for Jamesian criticism to run to abstraction is one of its weaknesses. Much of it is excessively concerned with tracing the schematic relations of moral themes: innocence, corruption, treachery and so forth. The Garden of Eden and the "sense of evil" play an exaggerated and sometimes unnecessary role in many recent interpretations. There have been some very interesting analyses of James's imagery, but some of these tend to be schematic in a way that is untrue to the impression the novels make on the reader. The most difficult task, and the most worthwhile one—that of rendering the sheer quality of James's writing—is not often attempted. The late manner especially needs an apologist, skilful enough as a writer to achieve his purpose without the wearisome textual analysis which would only serve still further to alienate the unconverted. To say the least, James is a vastly entertaining author, even in the books which have been labelled difficult. Not enough people are yet aware of the pleasure he can give them.

REFERENCES

1. *Henry James. The Untried Years*, p. 60.
2. *The Craft of Fiction*, p. 163.
3. *Op. cit.*, p. 164.
4. *The Triple Thinkers*, p. 104.
5. *Op. cit.*, p. 96
6. *The Complex Fate*, p. 79.
7. *Op. cit.*, pp. 79–80.
8. *G.T.*, p. 111.
9. *G.T.*, p. 161.
10. *G.T.*, p. 160.
11. *G.B.*, p. 520.
12. *G.B.*, p. 542.

BIBLIOGRAPHY

Note

*In all cases in which more than one edition of any work is listed,
all references in the text are to the edition marked* * *in this
Bibliography.*

I. HENRY JAMES

Fuller information may be found in *A Bibliography of Henry James*
by Leon Edel and Dan H. Laurence, 1957, to which the author is
much indebted in his compilation of the following lists.

Note on the "New York" and "Standard" editions. In 1907–09 the New
York edition of James's Novels and Tales appeared in twenty-four
volumes, published by Charles Scribner's Sons. James made extensive revisions for this edition, and also wrote eighteen prefaces, one
for each novel and one for each volume of stories. Many of his works
were excluded, e.g. *The Europeans, Washington Square, The Bostonians,*
and a considerable number of stories.

In 1921–23 Percy Lubbock's edition of the Novels and Stories
appeared in thirty-five volumes, published by Macmillan and Co.
Ltd., London. This, for convenience, is here referred to as the Standard Edition. It is based on the New York edition, but it contains
works which had been excluded from the latter, e.g. the novels listed
above, and a number of stories. It does not include *The Ivory Tower*
and *The Sense of the Past,* which had been added to the New York
edition. *The Other House* and *The Outcry* are excluded. Of the stories
not included almost all are covered by the two following collections:

Travelling Companions, with foreword by Albert Mordell, New York
1919; and *Eight Uncollected Tales,* ed. with introd. by Edna Kenton,
New Brunswick, N.J., 1950.

1. Novels

Watch and Ward, in *Atlantic Monthly,* XXVIII, 1871. Book publication:
　　Boston 1878.
Roderick Hudson, here cited as *R.H.,* in *Atlantic Monthly,* XXXV–XXXVII,
　　1875. Book publication: Boston 1875; first Eng. edn. London
　　1879. Edn. cited (see note above): *Chiltern Library, John
　　Lehmann, London 1947.
The American, here cited as *Am.,* in *Atlantic Monthly,* XXXVII–XXXIX,
　　1876–77. Book publication: Boston 1877; London 1877.
　　*Chiltern Library, John Lehmann, London 1949.

The Europeans, in *Atlantic Monthly*, XLII, 1878. Book publication: London 1878; Boston 1878.

Confidence, in *Scribner's Monthly*, XVIII–XIX, 1879–80. Book publication: London 1879; Boston 1880.

Washington Square, in *Cornhill Magazine*, XLI–XLII, and Harper's *New Monthly Magazine*, LXI–LXII, 1880. Book publication: New York 1880; London 1881.

The Portrait of a Lady, here cited as *P.L.*, in *Macmillan's Magazine*, XLII–XLV and *Atlantic Monthly*, XLVI–XLVIII, 1880–81. Book publication: London 1881; Boston and New York 1881. *World's Classics, O.U.P., London 1947.

The Bostonians, here cited as *B.*, in *Century Magazine*, XXIX–XXXI, 1885–86. Book publication: London 1886; New York 1886. *Chiltern Library, Lehmann, London 1952.

The Princess Casamassima, here cited as *P.C.*, in *Atlantic Monthly*, LVI–LVIII, 1885–86. Book publication: London and New York 1886. *Chiltern Library, John Lehmann, London 1948.

The Reverberator, in *Macmillan's Magazine*, LVII–LVIII, 1888. Book publication: London and New York 1888. *St. Edn.

The Tragic Muse, here cited as *T.M.*, in *Atlantic Monthly*, LXIII–LXV, 1889–90. Book publication: Boston and New York 1890; first Eng. edn. London 1890. *St. Edn.

The Other House, in *Illustrated London News*, CIX, 1896. Book publication: London 1896; New York 1896.

The Spoils of Poynton, here cited as *S.P.*, in *Atlantic Monthly*, LXXVII–LXXVIII, 1896, with title *The Old Things*. Book publication: London 1897; Boston and New York 1897. *Chiltern Library, John Lehmann, London 1947.

What Maisie Knew, here cited as *W.M.K.*, in *Chap Book*, VI–VII, and *New Review*, XVI–XVII, 1897. Book publication: London 1897; Chicago and New York 1897. *Chiltern Library, John Lehmann, London 1947.

The Awkward Age, in *Harper's Weekly*, XLII–XLIII, 1898–99. Book publication: London 1899; New York 1899.

The Sacred Fount. New York 1901; London 1901.

The Wings of the Dove, here cited as *W.D.* New York 1902; London 1902. *St. Edn.

The Ambassadors, here cited as *Amb.*, in *North American Review*, CLXXVI–CLXXVII, 1903. Book publication: London 1903; New York 1903. *Everyman Library, Dent, London 1947.

The Golden Bowl, here cited as *G.B.* New York 1904; London 1905. *Methuen, London 1956.

The Outcry. London 1911; New York 1911.

The Ivory Tower. London 1917; New York 1917.

The Sense of the Past. London 1917; New York 1917.

2. Stories referred to in the text

The title of the relevant volume in the Standard edition
is added in brackets.

"A Passionate Pilgrim," in *Atlantic Monthly*, xxvii, 1871. (*St. edn. *The Reverberator*, etc., here cited as *R*.)

"The Madonna of the Future," in *Atlantic Monthly*, xxxi, 1873. (*St. edn. *R*.)

"Madame de Mauves," in *Galaxy*, xvii, 1874. (*St. edn. *R*.)

"Daisy Miller," in *Cornhill Magazine*, xxxvii–xxxviii, 1878. (*St. edn. *Daisy Miller*, etc., here cited as *D.M*.)

"An International Episode," in *Cornhill Magazine*, xxxviii–xxxix, 1878–79. (St. edn. *Lady Barbarina*, etc., here cited as *L.B*.)

"The Pension Beaurepas," in *Atlantic Monthly*, xliii, 1879. (St. edn. *L.B*.)

"A Bundle of Letters," in *Parisian*, No. 38, 1879. (St. edn. *L.B*.)

"The Point of View," in *Century Magazine*, xxv, 1882. (St. edn. *L.B*.)

"Lady Barbarina," in *Century Magazine*, xxviii, 1884. (*St. edn. *L.B*.)

"The Path of Duty," in *English Illustrated Magazine*, ii, 1884. (St. edn. *The Diary of a Man of Fifty*, etc.)

"The Liar," in *Century Magazine*, xxxvi, 1888. (St. edn. *The Aspern Papers*, etc.)

"The Aspern Papers," in *Atlantic Monthly*, lxi, 1888. (St. edn. *The Aspern Papers*, etc.)

"The Lesson of the Master," in *Universal Review*, i, 1888. (St. edn. *The Lesson of the Master*, etc., here cited as *L.M*.)

"The Private Life," in *Atlantic Monthly*, lxix, 1892. (St. edn. *The Altar of the Dead* etc.) *Selected Stories by Henry James*, World's Classics, O.U.P. 1957, here cited as *S.S.*

"The Real Thing," in *Black and White*, iii, 1892. (St. edn. *D.M.*) *S.S.*

"The Middle Years," in *Scribner's Magazine*, xiii, 1893. (St. edn. *L.M*.)

"The Death of the Lion," in *Yellow Book*, i, 1894. (*St. edn. *L.M.*)

"The Coxon Fund," in *Yellow Book*, ii, 1894. (*St. edn. *L.M.*)

"The Next Time," in *Yellow Book*, vi, 1895. (St. edn. *L.M.*)

"The Turn of the Screw," in *Collier's Weekly*, xx–xxi, 1898. (St. edn. *The Aspern Papers*, etc.)

"Broken Wings," in *Century Magazine*, lxi, 1900. (St. edn. *The Author of Beltraffio*, etc.) *S.S.*

"The Two Faces," in *Harper's Bazaar*, xxxiii, 1900. (St. edn. *The Aspern Papers*, etc.) *S.S.*

"The Beast in the Jungle," in *The Better Sort*, London 1903; New York 1903. (St. edn. *The Altar of the Dead*, etc.) *Fourteen Stories by Henry James*, selected by David Garnett, London 1947.

"The Jolly Corner," in *English Review*, I, 1908. (St. edn. *The Altar of the Dead*, etc.)

"A Round of Visits," in *English Review*, v, 1910. (St. edn. *Maud Evelyn*, etc.)

3. Plays

The Complete Plays of Henry James, ed. Leon Edel, New York and London 1949. The editor's introduction is an indispensable treatment of James's dramatic work.

4. Travel Books

A Little Tour in France, in *Atlantic Monthly*, LII–LIII, 1883–84, with title *En Province*. Book publication: Boston 1884; first Eng. edn. London 1900.

English Hours, here cited as *E.H.* London 1905. These essays had appeared before in periodicals, many also in book form.

The American Scene. London 1907; New York 1907. Most of it had appeared before in periodicals.

Italian Hours. London 1909 Like *English Hours* this is a collection of essays which had appeared before in periodicals, many also in book form.

5. Criticism

The Art of the Novel. Critical Prefaces by Henry James, with introd. by R. P. Blackmur. New York 1934; London 1935.

The Scenic Art. Notes on Acting and the Drama 1872–1901, ed. with introd. and notes by Allan Wade. New Brunswick, N.J. 1948; London 1949.

The American Essays, ed. with introd. by Leon Edel. New York 1956.

The Painter's Eye. Notes and Essays on the Pictorial Arts, selected and ed. by John L. Sweeney. London 1956; Cambridge, Mass. 1956.

The House of Fiction, ed. with introd. by Leon Edel. London 1957.

Literary Reviews and Essays on American, English and French Literature, ed. Albert Mordell. New York 1957. Includes more than sixty essays and reviews from the first twenty years of James's literary life.

6. Biography

Hawthorne. London 1879; New York 1880.

William Wetmore Story and his Friends, here cited as *W.W.S.* Edinburgh and London 1903; New York 1903. *London 1957.

7. Autobiography

A Small Boy and Others. New York 1913; London 1913.

Notes of a Son and Brother. New York 1914; London 1914.

The Middle Years. London 1917; New York 1917.

Henry James: Autobiography, ed. with introd. and notes by F. W. Dupee, here cited as *H.J.A.* *London 1956; New York 1956. The three autobiographical works listed above are here published together.

8. Letters

The Letters of Henry James, selected and ed. by Percy Lubbock, 2 vols., here cited as *L.* *London 1920; New York 1920.

Theatre and Friendship. Some Henry James letters with a Commentary by Elizabeth Robins. *London 1932; New York 1932.

Henry James and Robert Louis Stevenson. A Record of Friendship and Criticism, ed. with introd. by Janet Adam Smith. London 1948.

The Selected Letters of Henry James, ed. with introd. by Leon Edel. New York 1955; *London 1956.

Henry James and H. G. Wells. A Record of their Friendship, their Debate on the Art of Fiction, and their Quarrel, ed. with introd. by Leon Edel and Gordon N. Ray. London 1958.

9. Notebooks

The Notebooks of Henry James, ed. with introd. by F. O. Matthiessen and Kenneth B. Murdock. New York and London 1947.

10. Miscellaneous

Within the Rim and Other Essays. London 1919.

II. OTHERS

This selection of books and articles dealing with James's life and work is of necessity very limited. For fuller materials Lyon N. Richardson's bibliographical list in *The Question of Henry James*, ed. F. W. Dupee, 1945, cited here as *Q.H.J.*, and that of Maurice Beebe and William T. Stafford in *Modern Fiction Studies*, III. 1 (Spring 1957) may be recommended.

What may seem a disproportionate number of articles on *The Golden Bowl* are included here to illustrate points made on this controversial novel in Chapter VII.

ALLOTT, MIRIAM: "Symbol and Image in the Later Work of Henry James," in *Essays in Criticism*, III (July 1953), pp. 321 ff.

——: "Henry James and the Fantasticated Conceit: *The Sacred Fount*," in *The Northern Miscellany*, 1953, pp. 76 ff.

ANDERSON, QUENTIN: *The American Henry James.* New Brunswick, N.J. 1957; London 1958.

BARZUN, JAQUES: "Henry James, Melodramatist," in *Q.H.J.*, pp. 254 ff.

BEACH, JOSEPH WARREN: *The Method of Henry James.* New Haven 1918; London 1918.

BEWLEY, MARIUS: *The Complex Fate.* *London 1952; New York 1954.

——: *The Eccentric Design. Form in the Classic American Novel.* London 1959; New York 1959.

BLACKMUR, R. P.: "Henry James," in *Literary History of the United States*, ed. R. E. Spiller and others. New York 1948, VOL. II, pp. 1039 ff.

——: "In the Country of the Blue," in *Q.H.J.*, pp. 191 ff.

——: "The Loose and Baggy Monsters of Henry James," in *The Lion and the Unicorn*, London 1955, pp. 268 ff; New York 1955.

BROOKS, VAN WYCK: *The Pilgrimage of Henry James.* New York 1925.

CHASE, RICHARD: *The American Novel and its Tradition.* New York 1957; London 1958.

DUPEE, F. W.: *The Question of Henry James: A Collection of Critical Essays*, ed. F. W. Dupee. New York 1945; London 1947.

——: *Henry James.* New York 1951; London 1951.

EDEL, LEON: *Henry James. The Untried Years, 1843–1870.* New York and Philadelphia 1953; London 1953.

——: Introductory essay to *The Sacred Fount.* New York 1953; London 1959.

ELIOT, T. S.: "Henry James." First pub. 1918; in **Q.H.J.*, pp. 123 ff.

FIREBAUGH, J. J.: "The Ververs," in *Essays in Criticism*, IV (October 1954), pp. 400 ff.

GODDARD, HAROLD C.: "A Pre-Freudian Reading of *The Turn of the Screw*," with Prefatory Note by Leon Edel, in *Nineteenth Century Fiction*, XII, July 1957, pp. 1 ff.

GOSSE, SIR EDMUND: "Henry James," in *Aspects and Impressions*, London 1922, pp. 28 ff.

KELLEY, CORNELIA P.: *The Early Development of Henry James.* Univ. of Illinois Studies in Language and Literature, VOL. XV, 1930.

KETTLE, ARNOLD: *An Introduction to the English Novel*, VOL. II, London 1953; New York 1960.

KNIGHT, L. C.: "Henry James and the Trapped Spectator," in *Explorations*, London 1946, pp. 155 ff.

KROOK, DOROTHEA: "The Golden Bowl," in *Cambridge Journal*, VII (Sept. 1954), pp. 716 ff.

LEAVIS, F. R.: *The Great Tradition*, here cited as *G.T.* *London 1948; New York 1948.

——: "The Novel as Dramatic Poem: *The Europeans*," in *Scrutiny*, XV (Spring 1948), pp. 209 ff.

——: "*What Maisie Knew*: A Disagreement by F. R. Leavis," in Marius Bewley: *The Complex Fate*, London 1952, pp. 114 ff.

LIDDELL, ROBERT: "The 'Hallucination' theory of *The Turn of the Screw*," in *A Treatise on the Novel*, London 1947, pp. 138 ff.

LUBBOCK, PERCY: *The Craft of Fiction.* London 1921; New York 1921.

MATTHIESSEN, F. O.: *American Renaissance: Art and Expression in the Age of Emerson and Whitman.* New York 1941.

——: *Henry James: The Major Phase.* London and New York 1944.

NOWELL-SMITH, SIMON: *The Legend of the Master,* compiled by Simon Nowell-Smith. London 1947; New York 1948.

NUHN, FERNER: *The Wind Blew from the East.* New York 1942.

PEACOCK, RONALD: "Henry James and the Drama," in *The Poet in the Theatre,* London 1946, pp. 21 ff; New York 1946.

POUND, EZRA: "Henry James." First pub. 1920; in *Literary Essays of Ezra Pound,* ed. with introd. by T. S. Eliot, London 1954, pp. 295 ff.

RAHV, PHILIP: "The Heiress of all the Ages," in *Image and Idea,* New York 1949, pp. 51 ff.

——: "Attitudes towards Henry James," in *Image and Idea,* New York 1949, pp. 77 ff. Also in *Q.H.J.,* pp. 280 ff.

ROURKE, CONSTANCE: *American Humour.* New York 1931.

SANDEEN, ERNEST: "*The Wings of the Dove* and *The Portrait of a Lady:* a Study of Henry James's later Phase," in *Publications of the Modern Language Association of America,* LXIX. 2 (Sept. 1954), pp. 695 ff.

SPENCER, JAMES L.: "Symbolism in James's *The Golden Bowl,*" in *Modern Fiction Studies,* III. 4 (Winter 1957–58), pp. 333 ff.

TATE, ALLEN: "Three Commentaries," in *Sewanee Review,* LVIII (Winter 1950), pp. 5 ff.

TRILLING, LIONEL: "The Princess Casamassima," in *The Liberal Imagination.* New York 1950; London 1951, pp. 58 ff.

——: "The Bostonians," in *The Opposing Self,* New York 1955; London 1955, pp. 104 ff.

WALSH, WILLIAM: "Maisie in *What Maisie Knew,*" in *The Use of Imagination,* London 1959, pp. 148 ff.

WEGELIN, CHRISTOF: "The Internationalism of *The Golden Bowl,*" in *Nineteenth Century Fiction,* XI (Dec. 1956), pp. 161 ff.

WHARTON, EDITH: *A Backward Glance.* New York and London 1934.

WILSON, EDMUND: "The Ambiguity of Henry James." First pub. 1934; with revisions in **The Triple Thinkers,* London 1952, pp. 89 ff.

WINTERS, YVOR: "Maule's Well, or Henry James and the Relation of Morals to Manners," in *Maule's Curse,* 1938; reprinted in *In Defence of Reason,* New York 1947, pp. 300 ff.